Choices

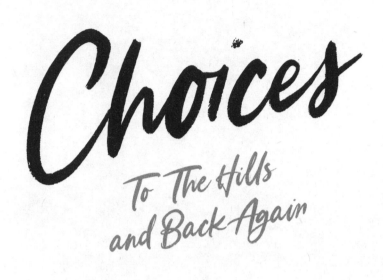

Choices
To The Hills and Back Again

AUDRINA PATRIDGE

GALLERY BOOKS

NEW YORK   LONDON   TORONTO   SYDNEY   NEW DELHI

Gallery Books
An Imprint of Simon & Schuster, Inc.
1230 Avenue of the Americas
New York, NY 10020

First Gallery Books hardcover edition July 2022

GALLERY BOOKS and colophon are registered trademarks of Simon & Schuster, Inc.

For information about special discounts for bulk purchases, please contact Simon & Schuster
Special Sales at 1-866-506-1949 or business@simonandschuster.com.

The Simon & Schuster Speakers Bureau can bring authors to your live event.
For more information or to book an event, contact the Simon & Schuster
Speakers Bureau at 1-866-248-3049 or visit our website at www.simonspeakers.com.

Interior design by Jaime Putorti

Manufactured in the United States of America

10 9 8 7 6 5 4 3 2 1

Library of Congress Cataloging-in-Publication Data is available.

ISBN 978-1-9821-8381-3
ISBN 978-1-9821-8383-7 (ebook)

For my parents, my siblings, and my friends,
who have stood by me through thick and thin

· Contents ·

Choices

· Introduction ·

The Power to Choose

When I first moved to Los Angeles, I imagined a life of excitement and adventure as I built a career in Hollywood, but I never could have imagined the incredible friendships, the once-in-a-lifetime experiences, and, yes, even the constant challenges and pressures that I would face. From the glamorous red-carpet events, to the cover of *Rolling Stone*, and countless hours on television—I have been on a journey that I could only have dreamed of as a little girl in Orange County in a church theater group. It's been an incredible and wild ride, and I know how lucky I am to have seen my dreams realized and then some. But there's more to the story.

If you see me on television, in the tabloids, or on social media—where millions of people follow along for glimpses into my life—you might think I've got it all figured out. A fresh blowout, a cool leather jacket, a beautiful sunset over the Pacific. It's such a lesson to never judge a book by the cover, or a celebrity by a tabloid picture. You never really know what's going on with someone.

Behind the practiced smile and the upbeat interview answers lies a depth of sadness few people know about. For several years, I hid the challenges I've faced, and now the carefully crafted façade is beginning to crack. I'm ready to share my story for better or worse. There's power in owning who you are, and I'm ready to step into my own as I recount the most fun, fulfilling, and wild years of my life—and some of the most difficult.

At age thirty-six, I'm a single mother trying to find my way, create an incredible life for my daughter, and build a fulfilling career. I finally know who I am—or, at least, I'm getting there. I've stripped away all of the posturing and pretending that defined my twenties, a time when I was learning who I was and what I wanted. I'm sure starring on a reality TV show watched by two million people every week didn't help that. But now that I've learned how to stand up for myself, I can never go back to saying yes to people and going with the flow if it means going against my heart. What a difference that mindset makes.

My life is full of love and joy in ways I couldn't imagine thanks to my beautiful, spirited daughter, Kirra. Sometimes I let myself daydream about the kind of woman she'll become. I often think she'll change the world. She's so full of love and strength, and she's so brave. I just know the combination will be unstoppable. When I look at Kirra, with her bright eyes, big smile, and open heart, I know that I need to tell my story. She is the reason I've become the woman I am today, like an angel sent from God.

And here's the funny thing: in trying to be strong and brave for Kirra, I learned to be strong and brave for myself too. I've been forced to know who I am and stand strong. I am just now stepping into my power as a woman, a mother, and an entrepreneur. Now I don't want to be silent anymore. I want to talk about the struggles, the missteps, the mistakes, including the regret of letting myself stay in a relationship that I knew was damaging for far too long. I work hard to make sure that Kirra's well-spoken and has a voice—that she's not afraid to speak her mind. I want her to advocate for herself as she grows up.

Writing my story has been a cathartic process. It has helped me to reclaim my power, to own this journey and all of its ups and downs. I share my story in hopes that it might help someone else struggling—whether it's in a toxic situation, abusive relationship, or any challenge that pushes you to know who you are and stand up for it. It's taken me a long while to peel away the layers of psychological and emotional manipulation and remember who I really am. I'm not ashamed of what I've been through; it has made me a stronger person in the end. It was the hardest fight of my life to get my power back. I've stopped giving in to the fears that I'm not good enough to be liked, valued, or heard. I've forgiven myself for staying in relationships that aren't working, for going along with what was easiest or would make other people happy. It's my greatest hope that this book will enable one woman to learn from my mistakes or take comfort in knowing that she's not alone.

I want to use my voice to make a difference and to inspire other women who are going through similarly tough situations or toxic relationships. I know what it's like to feel small, to be made small, and to have that smallness start to become your reality. I get so many messages from women who are stuck, and who want to know how I found the strength to change my life. Unfortunately, there's no secret. There's just the belief that you are enough to be worth fighting for. It's so simple. But somehow, in our darkest moments, it can be the hardest thing in the world to see the light and sprint toward it.

I am more blessed than I can say with a beautiful daughter and a career that has opened doors and led to countless opportunities. And that's what I choose to focus on each day. I choose to live in the light, to embrace the beauty of a sunny afternoon spent playing in the backyard with Kirra or walking along the beach near our home in Orange County. I'm stronger now because of what I've been through and the hard lessons I've learned. Like a diamond created under intense, unimaginable pressure, I am as strong as I've ever been and I'm ready to shine.

That's the life I want for us: one of abundance and happiness. I try to teach Kirra my mantra: "*You* have the power to choose!" I want her to know that she decides her future. We all do. I've given my power away for too long, and this book is one more step toward reclaiming it.

Every choice we make in our lives is creating who we are. I made a choice to move to Los Angeles, and I ended up on the reality TV show that would open so many doors and create a springboard to explore my passions. With every risk and every hurdle comes the big possibility that you'll fail. So what? Stumbling and falling is how you learn to catch yourself—to rebuild, to grow, and to never let falling keep you down. We have the power to choose the way we see the world, and I, for one, choose hope.

· *Chapter One* ·

From Orange County to *The Hills*

*R*eality television would come to shape my entire life—for better or worse—and bring me some of the greatest opportunities I could ever dream of. And yet, I didn't grow up watching reality television. When I was a teenager, my favorite shows were *Dawson's Creek* (team Pacey, for the record!) and *Felicity*. I watched *TRL* every day after school, and I watched hours and hours of MTV music videos.

When I look back on my simple, family-oriented childhood in Orange County, it's sort of surprising that I would come to find myself on reality TV for most of my adult life. I grew up in Yorba Linda, a very laid-back suburban community twenty minutes from the beach. My mom was a stay-at-home mom and my dad is an engineer for our family business, which makes mechanical parts for big companies to use on anything from airplanes to rides at Disneyland, from huge oil rigs to huge factory machinery for Coca-Cola.

My mom was not the PTA, baking cookies kind of mom. She was the outgoing, funny one that all of my friends love. She was fun and open, and my house was the hangout for most of my friends and my siblings' friends too. It was often a full house with me and my three younger siblings: my sisters, Casey and Samantha, and my brother, Mark. My mom also let us kids decorate our rooms however we wanted, so at one point, I had all four walls of my room painted different bright colors like a giant Rubik's cube. I love that she let us express ourselves like that. Geographically, my hometown's not that far from LA, but spiritually, it's a whole different planet. I loved growing up in a such a quiet, tight-knit town. A few years ago, I moved back to Orange County with my daughter because I want her to be raised in that same slower-paced, family-friendly environment.

My mom went over-the-top when it came to celebrations and threw us all these elaborate, themed parties. My favorites were my thirteenth-birthday "luau" with real fire dancers, and my eighteenth Vegas-themed party with craps and poker tables set up around our backyard to look like a real casino. I've started doing the same thing for Kirra, staging big, fun-themed birthday parties, which she seems to love—especially her mermaid-themed third birthday, complete with a sequined mermaid tail and an appearance by a "real" mermaid.

We went to church most Sundays as a family, all dressed in our Sunday best, my sisters and I with our hair done and dresses on. I liked going to church as a kid. I felt like it gave me the basis for my values and taught me where to turn when it feels like I have no one, which is to God. I tried the church's theater group too, and it was great place to explore my love of performing. Ever since I was little, I've always been intrigued by acting and performing. I remember being five or six and watching *The Mickey Mouse Club*, and I would always tell my mom that I was going to be on that TV one day. I knew at a young age that's what I wanted to do. So in high school, I started going to acting classes, and my mom really supported me with that. I was kind of shy growing up, but I broke out of it and pushed myself out of my comfort zone to pursue acting.

I honestly never liked high school. I went there to learn and I worked hard to do my homework during my lunch break so I could leave school at school. I looked forward to coming home and spending time with my family, or doing other activities like dance and theater. I even loaded up on my classes during my first three years of high school, so by senior year, I was at school only three hours a day and I could work afterward.

Don't get me wrong: I had a lot of friends in high school. I was friendly with everyone, and didn't get caught up in the drama or gossip. My mom told me that I wasn't allowed to have a boyfriend or wear makeup until I was sixteen years old, so for much of high school, I was skinny, underdeveloped, and fresh-faced, looking much younger than I was. I would definitely call it an awkward phase. I was fine with her rules, though, and I didn't rebel. I wasn't really interested in having a boyfriend at that age. I had crushes growing up, but I was mostly focused on other things, like dance and the swim team, where I swam the 400-yard freestyle.

My favorite classes in high school were science (especially biology) and art (drawing and painting). At the time, I thought about going to school to become a psychologist. I was always listening to my friends share their problems, giving advice and trying to help. People came to me, so it felt natural to think about ways to turn that into a career. I couldn't always take my own advice, but my friends appreciated my insightful, nonjudgmental words of wisdom. I've always been interested in why people are the way they are. I still think about that sometimes, especially when I'm in the waiting room at an audition looking at all the other girls there. Everyone has their own story and brings something unique to the role. You can take the same script, and ten different women are going to read it ten different ways. That's always fascinated me.

As soon as we got our driver's licenses, my friends and I went to shows every chance we got. I had always loved music, and during high school I got into the punk music scene. I even wanted to look the part, with my hair dyed purple and my nose pierced. Almost every weekend, my friends and I would go to the best venues in the area—The Glass House, Observatory, and Chain Reaction—to hear our favorite bands, including Thrice, Finch, Rufio, and Yellowcard. We would dance and sing our hearts out and then rush home before our 10 p.m. curfew. I also worked at a small recording studio in Newport Beach during my senior year of high school, an experience that would serve me well when I got to LA.

After high school graduation, I started taking classes at Orange County Community College at night, and in the daytime I would go to LA to audition for commercials, music videos, and modeling gigs. Starting at sixteen years old, I took acting classes once a week in LA with a well-known acting coach named Fawn Irish. I also met with a modeling agent who often knew about commercial and acting gigs. I was soon going on lots of auditions—most actors spend more time auditioning for jobs than actually filming!—but it was in my acting classes more than anywhere else that I saw the real artistry behind the career. The other actors in my class were passionate and intense. They put everything they had into a scene, and I so admired their dedication to constant improvement. It was just incredible to watch them, and then to be able to get up there and act with them myself. It was so different from the church theater experience growing up!

As much as I loved it, there were parts of the process that took a bit of getting used to. For example, when I went out for roles, the other young women in the waiting room all looked exactly like me, with straight brown hair, the same thin frame, and about the same age. It was disheartening to see how many women were vying for the same roles in commercials or music videos. I landed roles in a few music videos for rock bands, none of which you've heard of. I loved music, so it was fun, and it certainly provided the opportunity to exercise my dramatic muscle. Plus, I got paid a hundred bucks for each, which was great at the time.

It was hectic running around LA all day from audition to audition, and the traffic was so unpredictable driving the forty miles back to Orange County for school. I was late to class so often that a couple of professors threatened to fail me. So I had to make a decision: stay in school and focus on my studies to try to become a psychologist, or move to LA and pursue acting and modeling full-time. I figured I could always reenroll in school and get back to my studies, but this was the time to give my dreams a shot, so I took the leap.

Thankfully, my parents were supportive of me leaving school and giving myself a real chance with the auditions. They knew I was serious from the acting classes I had taken in high school, but more than anything, they knew I had to get it out of my system—whether I found work or not. They understood the importance of not living a life with regrets and what-ifs.

I packed up my childhood bedroom, withdrew from my classes, and moved to LA to see what would happen. You know how some things are just meant to be? I think that I had to be in just the right place, at just the right time, for everything to work out as it did.

I was in LA with my dad looking for apartments in the Villas apartment complex, but unfortunately they didn't have a one-bedroom unit available. We were on our way out when I started chatting with two sweet girls in the elevator. They were both from Kansas, best friends, living in a three-bedroom and looking for a roommate. They overheard us talking about not finding a place, and offered me the room on the spot! It was a great apartment, and they seemed so normal and nice. My room would be very private, with its own bathroom. I couldn't believe how everything was already just clicking into place. I looked around and said, "When can I move in?" Just like that, I had my first apartment in LA.

Unfortunately, it wouldn't turn into a lifelong friendship. Once I got cast on *The Hills*, the girls turned a little sour toward me, and I moved into the next one-bedroom that became available in the building. But still—I was in LA and ready for anything!

I started my new life, mostly by enjoying the pool at my new apartment complex. There was nothing better than lying poolside and learning my lines for an upcoming audition. Believe it or not, that's where I met MTV producer Adam DiVello, who was there to scout the apartment complex for Lauren Conrad and Heidi Montag because they were moving from San Francisco where they both had attended the Academy of Art University for one semester. Lauren was getting a *Laguna Beach* spin-off show that was still in development. At the time, I had never watched Lauren on TV, but I knew who she was from magazines and interviews.

At first, when Adam approached me and introduced himself, I thought he was just another cheesy producer trying to hit on me or invite me to an "exclusive club" that night. But he talked about the shows he worked on, and I began to think he could be legit. He asked why I'd moved to LA, where I was from, and where I was working. I told him I'd recently started a job as a receptionist at Quixote Studios, a photo, video, and event studio in town that was the location of magazine and commercial shoots, music videos, fashion events . . . you name it. I needed to work and make money for rent and acting classes, and it seemed like a great place to get insight into some elements of the business. I could see the wheels turning in Adam's head as I told him that I'd already met some cool new people, including some amazing photographers and casting directors, through this job. I had been going out in LA for a few years already, and I knew the hottest spots to go each night of the week. Adam liked that I was in the know and could bring Lauren and Heidi out with me.

Adam told me he was moving quickly to put together this spin-off show, and just a few days later, I was in the MTV offices to meet the rest of the showrunners and producers. I shared the basics about myself and learned more about the show. They told me that, based on my background and the time they spent getting to know me, they thought I would be a great fit with the group of girls. I was in LA to pursue modeling and acting, and I quickly realized that this could be good practice for me to get comfortable in front of the camera. I didn't have a lot of expectations beyond that and really didn't know what I was in for, at all. Within a week or two, I signed the papers, and we started filming within two to three weeks.

I really credit my two bosses at Quixote Studios, Monica Mac-Donald and Jordan Kitaen, for being so supportive and encouraging when their new receptionist got offered a reality show. Not only did they encourage me from day one, but they also looked through my new contract to make sure it was sound and reasonable. Monica went even further, saying that MTV could film there, which would allow my two jobs to coexist so much more easily. Of course, she also warned me not to let this interrupt my real job. I would, after all, be a receptionist whenever I was working, not a "reality TV star." The job still needed to get done, and the filming couldn't undermine my performance at work. That all sounded fair to me.

I didn't know if the show would last or what would become of my reality television debut, so I wasn't rushing to leave my exciting job at Quixote. I was gaining insights into the business, just like Lauren, Whitney Port, and Heidi were forging their ways in fashion magazines and publicity, respectively.

The show followed the personal and professional lives of four young women living in LA—Lauren, Heidi, Whitney, and me. Lauren was very much the star of the show, and we were her friends and supporting cast. Coming off the buzz of *Laguna Beach*, *The Hills* premiered to a fan base eager to find out what Lauren was up to next. And we were thrilled to see the following only grow from there as the real-world issues of us trying to figure out our careers and love lives resonated with viewers so strongly. As we kept shooting, Heidi and I each got to film more of our own lives and see our journeys captured more. It never bothered me that the spotlight was on Lauren; it was her spin-off from *Laguna Beach*.

When the show started, Lauren was interning at *Teen Vogue* in the fashion closet, alongside Whitney Port, who was in college at the time. Lauren and Heidi were taking classes together at the Fashion Institute of Design and Merchandising, after both transferring from the Academy of Art University in San Francisco.

After a few weeks of classes, Heidi dropped out and got a job as an assistant at Bolthouse Productions, where she learned the ropes of event planning.

We all filmed our professional lives as well as our personal lives, showing the office dynamics, work challenges, and boss interactions we were grappling with. After we wrapped the first season of the show, I decided to move on from my job at Quixote Studios. As I thought about what I wanted to do next, I was eager to dive into my passions, so I looked for a new opportunity in the music industry. I landed a job as an A&R assistant at Epic Records, where I worked for a few years during the filming of the second through fifth seasons of the show. I got to meet great bands, go to shows regularly like my high school days, and use my knowledge of the music scene. Part of my job was listening to demo tapes sent in by bands all over the world. I sorted them into "yes," "no," and "maybe" piles as I identified the acts with the most talent and potential. It was also great for *The Hills* to film me going to shows and hanging out with bands, like Good Charlotte, Red Jumpsuit Apparatus, and The Script. This was the beginning of factoring the good of the show into my own life decisions.

The Hills became a reality TV and pop culture phenomenon that landed us on the cover of *Rolling Stone* magazine, among many others, and in the zeitgeist for most of my twenties. We were covered regularly by every tabloid magazine and drew some of MTV's highest-ever ratings. Lauren went from interning at *Teen Vogue* to being on the cover.

Once I signed on to the show, I wasn't allowed to go to the pool for two weeks, until we officially started filming, because the producers wanted me to meet Heidi and Lauren "organically" on-camera. I don't know how natural our first meeting actually was, considering the producers scheduled it during my lunch break at work, but I gamely raced home from Quixote Studios, threw on a bathing suit, and headed out to the pool where Heidi was already lying out. Then we just struck up a conversation. Heidi seemed immediately easy to talk to, but Lauren was a little harder to read.

In the very beginning, Lauren didn't seem very open to getting to know us. She seemed a little quiet and withdrawn, and now, with years of reality TV experience under my belt, I understand why she was so apprehensive to let people in right away. I've come to learn that you never know who is using you or who will turn on you to get their fifteen minutes in the spotlight—a lesson Lauren had probably already learned while filming *Laguna Beach*. Heidi was the total opposite. She was super friendly and outgoing, immediately jumping into sharing and making plans. Heidi and I began to hang out off-camera too. When we first started filming, she would come to my apartment for a drink and we would talk for hours, or we would go out dancing for the night. We definitely hit it off right off the bat! We hung out a lot when Lauren was dating her longtime boyfriend Jason Wahler (the one she chose over Paris, for you megafans!) because she was around less.

And that was the beginning: starting in 2006, I spent five years discovering myself, surviving bad dates, gaining and losing friendships, and exploring new ambitions—all while filming *The Hills*.

When we started filming, it was definitely a learning curve for me. I wasn't used to people watching and listening to every conversation and every dinner or coffee date with friends. But there is nothing more awkward and strange than filming a date with a new guy. It completely changes the evening. We can't just show up at a restaurant and find a table; it's much more involved than that. Typically, when my date and I would arrive, the production crew would mic us, and then we'd each get filmed walking into the restaurant, sometimes multiple times if they needed different angles or lighting changes. When we finally sat at our table and could actually talk to each other, we were often interrupted to change the lighting or adjust a camera, and we might be asked to repeat something. It was a little nerve-racking at first, because you're already nervous going on a date with someone. Can you imagine how awkward it is to be on a first date with bright lights in your face and cameras everywhere? Sometimes we would start talking about how awkward it was, and that part is always cut out of the show, obviously. Once Heidi and Lauren had boyfriends, I was the one who always went on dates, and I started to learn how to be in my own little bubble, ignore the cameras and lights, and just focus on what's in front of me.

Don't forget that while we were filming in a restaurant, there were people all around us just trying to have dinner. Once they saw the lights and multiple cameras, they would start staring at us. And then eventually, when *The Hills* became more widely known, if we were out filming, fans would stand behind the camera and film us or take pictures. Production always got so annoyed!

As the show gained viewers and popularity, it became a cultural conversation, part of the trend at the time toward reality television. MTV even created an aftershow to rehash the episodes for fans, hosted by *Schitt's Creek* star Dan Levy. We could feel that it was catching on very quickly. When I was out running errands or with friends, fans started coming up to me at stores or restaurants to say hello. Women in their teens or twenties would tell me they watched the show and really felt like they could relate to me with my situation with Justin Bobby or my rocky friendship with Lauren. Once a girl came up to me at the airport and started screaming and crying, asking if she could give me a hug. I found myself hugging a stranger, who was crying at the chance to meet me. I couldn't wrap my head around it. It was so surreal. These women who related to me in some way made me feel so good about doing the show and sharing so much of my life. I would try to tell them: just learn from my mistakes.

The first couple interactions like this made me realize that even though they watched me through the TV, the show's viewers truly felt like they knew me. Sometimes I could get down on myself for how the Justin situation was being portrayed on the show. I would start to question myself and my place on the show and feel incredibly stupid—I mean, how would you feel if all of your greatest dating regrets were broadcast for everyone to see? But then I would meet a fan who would say that I was actually inspiring them as they were going through the same thing. It made me feel like I was helping people realize they weren't alone.

It's funny to think that in a weird, roundabout way, this is kind of what I wanted to accomplish by being a psychologist too.

We were also invited to so many awards shows, and even asked to present a few times. I'll never forget the 2007 MTV Video Music Awards, in particular. Lauren, Whitney, and I were onstage to present the award for Male Artist of the Year. Lauren and Whitney were beyond excited when Justin Timberlake won, because they were superfans. His wasn't my kind of music, so I couldn't have cared less, but I was excited for them. And then Justin wouldn't even come up to us and accept the award in front of a packed house! Chris Brown came up onstage with him, took the award from us himself, and then presented it to Justin as we backed off to the side. The girls were devastated, and I was annoyed at his rude, diva behavior. And then, as if that wasn't bad enough, Justin took center stage and said to the crowd: "MTV, play more damn videos. We don't want to see *The Simpsons* or reality television." It was such a personal attack on us! Lauren's jaw just dropped. We were humiliated.

Fortunately, not everyone was as rude. Our table was right next to this up-and-coming artist and her mom. Maybe you recognize the name Rihanna? I spent a while chatting with her and her mom that night, and she couldn't have been nicer. She was probably one of my favorite people I've ever met at an awards show.

Another year at the Teen Choice Awards, *The Hills* won an award for Celebrity Reality TV, and Lauren and I accepted the award. When we won, I think the two of us sat there in shock until they called our names again before we realized we had to go up onstage and accept this giant surfboard. That one was really meaningful to win, because it was decided by the fans.

I eventually got used to presenting at awards shows. After hosting red carpets and working on live TV, I finally learned how to set my nerves aside and jump into performance mode as I made my way onto the stage. At the very last minute, right before going up onstage to present, I tended to get butterflies. I would get super quiet and in my head, but I'd always remember to take a deep breath. Somehow, it always made all of those feelings fade into the background. I would just do the best I could to have fun with it. As soon as I walked out onstage, I was able to focus and calm down.

The funny thing is, I didn't know about stylists at the time, so either I always dressed myself, or I worked with a designer's showroom to borrow a dress. I started making friends with a lot of the showroom people, so that anytime there was an event, they would help dress me. Thankfully, at a photo shoot, I met my good friend Joey, who was the stylist on-set. We hit it off immediately, and ever since then she's dressed me for red carpets. She knows my style, which is a little bit edgy, a little rock-and-roll, and a little sexy.

By the end of the third season, *The Hills* was the highest-rated cable show of 2008. We were up to twenty-eight episodes per season, and the pressure was mounting to create more storylines and amp up the drama. We were becoming experts at the club confrontation, cocktail in hand, or the quiet one-on-one, often accompanied by a few tears. The show continued to shift and change shape as our relationships changed. During the fourth season, Whitney moved to New York to work at Diane von Furstenberg and got her own spin-off, *The City*. We were starting to feel rumblings that other cast changes could happen too, but for a while still, we were just enjoying the ride.

· Chapter Two ·

Lights, Camera, Reality

The success of *The Hills* was opening so many doors for all of us. Lauren was working on her fashion line and landed a book deal for a series of novels. I was pursuing my career as an actress and model. Heidi and Spencer Pratt got married, which was filmed for our fifth season. We were definitely growing up and coming into our own. The question remained whether we could do it all together, on-air, without acknowledging the changes in our lives and the ubiquitous media glare that came as a result of the show's success. *The Hills* glossed over the attention we received or the way our lives changed as the show continued, unlike the way *Keeping Up with the Kardashians*, for example, includes the pressures and opportunities that come with their family's fame.

There were a lot of fun perks that came with being on a hit reality show, which *The Hills* quickly became. Companies would send us boxes of clothes and products in hopes we would be photographed wearing them. We were offered all of these free trips by hotels or travel companies to incredible locations like Tahiti, Bali, and Mexico, in exchange for a photo in a magazine—or sometimes just in hopes the paparazzi would follow. Now you have all of these Instagram influencers who do similar things, but ten years ago, that market didn't exist. It was all about reality TV stars, and the hope that whatever they did would be picked up on the show.

I also gained access to the incredible nightlife circuit exclusive to people in the entertainment industry. At a regular bar or club, it was difficult to have a few drinks and let loose with friends. You never knew who was around, who might be photographing you, or who might be waiting for you to let your guard down and pick a fight. But certain places were only for industry insiders, and they gave us a safe place to have fun and not worry about who was watching.

At the time, my favorite place to be was Hyde on the Sunset Strip in West Hollywood. It was a tiny club that could fit only about a hundred people max, but it was the place to be. I was going once or twice a week, if not more. There were strict "no cameras" and "no paparazzi" rules inside, so it became mysterious and exclusive. Everyone had to know someone in the business to get in, and there was an understanding and expectation of privacy. It became a place I genuinely looked forward to going to and having fun without worry. Hyde had a lounge-y vibe to it with deep leather booths and low tables, providing lots of privacy for small groups to hang out and dance to DJs like Samantha Ronson and Steve Aoki. And, of course, it was fun to party with some of the biggest names in town, including P. Diddy, Paris Hilton, Lindsay Lohan, Britney Spears, David Spade, and so many more. After Hyde's last call, the whole place would usually go back to someone's house for an after-hours party, often at Kevin Connolly's or Paris Hilton's, Ryan Cabrera's or Shane West's. We would keep the party going until the early morning, ordering food, mixing drinks, and taking turns with the playlist. The *Entourage* guys were big then, and Kevin Connolly and Adrian Grenier were always around and up for a good time. Kevin was a total ladies' man and super flirty with everyone. A few times, he chatted me up and tried to set up some plans for us to hang out, but I wasn't into it. He didn't seem bothered. He and his friends always seemed to be surrounded by gorgeous girls. You never knew what could happen at Hyde, or who would be there. I'll never forget one night when Lauren and I requested that the DJ play "Don't Stop Believin'" by Journey. When it came on, P. Diddy started belting it out right alongside us.

And then there were the *really* crazy experiences—like the time I got flown out to Vegas on a private jet by a prince who wanted a group of celebrities at his birthday. I was there with a few of my castmates from the film *Sorority Row*, as well as Megan Fox and Brian Austin Green, and even Leonardo DiCaprio.

After the birthday party, we all went to a club to hang out, and this bouncer kept coming over to me saying that Leo would like to get me a drink at his table. I looked over at his table, and he was just surrounded by supermodels. It was intimidating! I told the bouncer I would just finish my drink and then say hello. But I never went, even when the bouncer came back over a couple more times. So, Leo came over, sat down at our table alongside me, Megan, and Brian, and introduced himself to me. I told him I knew who he was, obviously, and we chatted for a while. He asked for my phone number, and we texted a little after the trip to Vegas, but we never actually hung out. Leo was very private, and with the constant filming for *The Hills* and the paparazzi attention, it just felt too tough to make anything work.

As incredible as the clubs and publicity opportunities were, nothing will top the thrill of being on the cover of *Rolling Stone*, one of the most iconic magazines in the world. This is the moment when you know your show matters—that you've made it. When my agent called with the news that they wanted the four of us— Lauren, Heidi, Whitney, and me—on the cover, I could hardly contain myself. *The Hills* had been on for two years, and this was an incredible compliment and testament to the attention it was getting. It was totally surreal, and I couldn't think about it too much without totally freaking out.

The inspiration for the shoot was the classic 1982 *Rolling Stone* cover of the girl group the Go-Go's. The four of us wore coordinating pale-pink underwear, and it was fun and playful. I actually knew the photographer from working at Quixote Studios, so the whole day was really lighthearted and comfortable. Even Lauren and Heidi, who were not speaking at the time, were able to put aside their drama and stay professional. Afterward, it was unbelievable to walk through the airport and see myself on the cover of *Rolling Stone* magazine, the May 15, 2008, issue to be exact. It was almost like a dream.

The incredible experience of filming *The Hills* wasn't without its drawbacks. I struggled to get used to the paparazzi following me everywhere. It was much less common for television personalities—as opposed to traditional actors—to be trailed by photographers when *The Hills* was first on the air, so the experience was strange and unnerving. Those were the days of up-the-skirt shots of Lindsay and Britney and Paris. It was intense, to say the least.

During the filming of season three when I lived with Lauren and Lo Bosworth, Lauren's best friend from high school who joined the cast in season two, we were followed anytime we left the house. We lived on a public street instead of in a gated apartment complex, and paparazzi would line up on the street just waiting for us to step outside. There was no privacy in the house either. We would lie out by the pool in the backyard, and photographers would peer over our fence. Lauren and Lo always parked in the gated driveway, but there were only two spots, so I had to park on the street. I ended up getting a parking ticket literally almost every day, and I was often photographed by the paparazzi plucking the ticket off my window.

The craziest experience of my time on *The Hills* happened on Rodeo Drive, when my friend Joey and I were shopping at Bloomingdale's. There were probably twenty paparazzi cars surrounding me as I got into my car and tried to drive away. One of the paparazzi cars hit the back of my car and took off, and another one chased after him. I was stuck, and I didn't know where to go. Once you're in your car trying to leave, they stand in front of you so you can't even pull out of your parking spot safely. They just crowd around your car with their cameras pressed up against your windows. The only way out is through, so I just inched forward slowly until they moved out of my way. The photographers held their cameras up to the windows trying to get a shot as I'm gritting my teeth and driving five miles per hour down Rodeo.

Some of the photographers would prioritize their shots over your basic safety. It was most dangerous at night because it was so tough to see where you were going with the flashes of their cameras. It's pretty scary to walk out of a club and have to hold your hand up to block the glare as you're trying to find your way to the valet or a car. Most of the time at bars and clubs open to the public, I never stayed out past midnight because everyone got more aggressive after that—the paparazzi, and even the fans. At some places, we would sneak out the back to avoid the paparazzi, even using decoys out front to distract them. Most photographers were just waiting to catch a photo of someone at their worst. But they weren't all bad. I became friendly with a few of the photographers I would see regularly. They were kind, and would occasionally give me a heads-up about other paparazzi coming or, after they got their shot, they would help divert them.

It's been a big topic of discussion whether *The Hills* was real or fake. The truth? It's somewhere in between, a little bit of both. A lot of what we did in terms of going to parties, bars, dinners, and events was real. Everything like that—the set pieces—was based in reality. Most of the time, the producers did not put on a fake party. Sometimes the intimate conversations, simmering tensions, or blowout fights that happened at those parties were instigated by production, and some were authentic. Nothing was scripted, so the words that we said and the things that we chose to do during those arguments were real either way. But me randomly running into somebody I was fighting with at a coffee shop so that we could fight some more? That wasn't so random.

Executive producers Tony DiSanto and Liz Gateley, the masterminds behind the show, have said pretty much the same thing: the friendships and tensions were real, but they pushed us to get bigger, more dramatic storylines. "We were really shooting year-round; the kids never got breaks," Liz said in an interview with ABC News ten years after *The Hills* finale. "We had to produce an episode a week. We did push them and we did have to make more story happen in a shorter amount of time. We sort of had to figure it out as we went."

The fictionalizing comes through in the creation of situations that would never naturally occur. Let's say I was having friction with Heidi. The production team would schedule me to film a coffee date with her, which of course I wouldn't have done in real life. And Heidi probably wouldn't have wanted to come, so she's annoyed she was forced to show up too. In this intimate, one-on-one conversation, in real life I might have just said: "Heidi, what's going on? Let's just get it all out in the open." But on the show, I felt this pressure to be confrontational, to create a scene that would be interesting to watch, and above all else, to give the producers what they wanted.

When you know going into a situation that the goal is to have a dramatic conversation with tension, conflict, and emotion, you kind of amplify your feelings. It wasn't necessarily about faking emotions, but rather turning up the intensity.

While the emotions may have been amped up, the settings and activities were all real life. We were filming almost year-round, with very little time off, so it would have been too difficult to plan so many parties and nights out just for the show. The big storylines were our real lives. We filmed with the people we were really dating, and we went to the clubs, bars, restaurants, and parties we would have been going to anyway.

Some of the greatest friendships of my life have come from *The Hills*. We had the opportunity to take a lot of amazing trips for the show to incredible places, including Hawaii and Costa Rica. There's nothing like putting us all together in a house or hotel to see what unfolds! We would travel as a group for a few days at a time, and it would all be edited into an episode. In addition to the booze and sometimes the drama, it was on these trips that friendships were made.

One of the most unexpected and beautiful friendships has been with Brody Jenner. I remember on a group trip to Costa Rica we stayed up all night, just the two of us. After an evening of partying, everybody went to bed at two in the morning, and we all had to be up at 6 a.m. to go to the airport. Brody and I both figured, what's three or four hours of sleep? So we sat by the pool, talking about everything, from relationships to music, from what we've been through in our lives to creative ideas, from current events to the future. We could sit for hours and never run out of things to say. Brody is so intelligent and we're both so passionate about many of the same things. We don't always agree, of course, but we enjoy debating back and forth with respect. That morning, as the sun rose over Costa Rica, the producers got up early in the morning and walked out to find us by the pool. They freaked! They said: "Oh my God, you guys are still together! We'll get the cameras!" Can't two people sit and talk in peace? They never ended up filming it, and it was nice to keep our friendship largely to ourselves.

I think what people don't know about Brody is that he has a sensitive side and he has the biggest heart. He always stands up for the people he loves, and for the person who can't stand up for themselves. He's very strong-willed and passionate, and also very opinionated. He doesn't put up with people's shit at all, and he doesn't hold back. I'm only recently realizing that I could have learned a lot from him in that regard.

We've always had a fun, flirty relationship, but we never took our friendship to that place. We both had other relationships going on, and we prioritized our friendship above any possible romantic feelings. It's only recently that we acknowledged that we both have had crushes on each other over the years.

Unfortunately, one connection that didn't last was my relationship with Lauren, who doesn't really talk to anyone from the old cast. There are reasons that she and I aren't friends anymore, and there was a lot of turmoil between us that we couldn't talk about on-camera at the time. It's what led to me moving out of the pool house out back when I lived with her and Lo, which might have seemed abrupt on the show, but in reality had been a long time coming. Lauren and I had the same agent and publicists, and it seemed to me that I was getting requests, opportunities, and gigs that our mutual agent was giving to Lauren instead. Yes, I blamed my agents for this, but it still wasn't great for my friendship with Lauren. I also found her to be very controlling over her friends. If you're in her circle, you have to do and say what Lauren does and says. Otherwise, you're on the outs. Heidi experienced the same thing. To an extent, I understand wanting to have control, especially in the reality TV world Lauren grew up in, when so much is controlled and decided for you. But there are limits. I (usually) had to do what the producers said—but I sure didn't have to obey Lauren.

There was also an issue with Justin that I just couldn't get over: Lauren acted like she hated Justin while the cameras were filming, but off-camera it seemed to be a different story. Once, when Justin was hanging out with me in the back house when I lived with Lauren and Lo, she even introduced Justin to her mom. When Justin and I were broken up, Lauren ran into him in Vegas and, according to a good friend of mine, ended up hooking up with him. When I heard this, I felt so betrayed.

The whole situation unfolded on the show, but neither of them would answer my calls or texts until the cameras were rolling. Apparently Lauren was saving her take for the cameras, and when we finally talked, she had it all twisted around to make me sound like I was delusional and out of my mind.

Then she got mad at *me*. Lauren and I were never really friends again.

Shortly after that, Lauren decided to leave the show, and we haven't talked since. Recently I took Kirra to see *Disney on Ice* and ran into Lauren and her sweet son. We said hello and chatted for a minute before moving on. There was absolutely no drama, and neither of us wanted to revisit the past. At this point, as grown-ups, we are not friends, but we are friendly if we run into each other. It would be silly to waste time on an old feud when we're with our families and our priorities are so clearly different now.

Justin never called me back about the Lauren situation after I reached out to talk, but he did agree to film and even though we continued to talk and film together on the show, that betrayal is lodged in the back of my head. The disrespect of him not acknowledging or legitimizing my feelings was almost as bad as the initial hookup itself. The show made it hard to walk away from someone like Justin completely, but that changed our dynamic for good.

It's a little unexpected, but I'm still friends with Kristin Cavallari (who replaced Lauren in season five, of course), and we stay in touch and text from time to time. Heidi and I went out to Nashville not long ago and filmed with her for her show, *Very Cavallari*. It was interesting to see how different her show was compared to *The Hills*. It was so real and raw, which means so completely unlike *The Hills*. When we went out together in Nashville and the cameras filmed us having the time of our lives, there was no acting involved. It was just three old best friends who hadn't seen each other in forever. We got to be ourselves, with no agenda or list of scenes we needed to film for the day.

From awards shows, to the cover of *Rolling Stone*, to fans coming up to me on the streets—*The Hills* has changed my life in so many ways. I am so glad I took that chance on my dreams and moved to LA.

· Chapter Three ·

The Ballad of Justin Bobby

*I*f there's one thing people ask me about without fail, it's my on-again, off-again relationship with the infamous Justin Bobby, the soulful bad boy who tugged on my heart for years on *The Hills*. Our tumultuous relationship was the source of so much fan speculation and gossip for more than a decade, in part thanks to the constant pressures of production and selective editing.

We met at nineteen, before *The Hills*, when Justin was an aspiring musician and hair stylist, and I was working as a receptionist at Quixote Studios, the huge studio space that hosted photography and video shoots for magazines, advertisements, and just about anything. Justin Brescia came to Quixote as the assistant to a team of hair stylists working on a big, top secret music video for Madonna. Even through all of the buzz that day, when I saw him, I just felt an instant connection.

He must have felt it too, because he kept walking back and forth in front of my desk all day, smiling or nodding to me. Every time, I asked, "Do you need help? Do you need something?" He would make up some little excuse, like he was looking for a magazine or asking which way the bathroom was. The barista was out when he asked about the coffee bar, so I told him I'd make him something. But I warned him: "If the phone rings, I've got to run and grab it." I offered him a latte or a cappuccino, or any of the coffee drinks on our menu, but instead of reading it, he was looking at me. He said, "I'll have whatever you would have." Since I don't drink coffee, I gave him my favorite Odwalla blueberry juice. He took it and drank it—even though I later found out he hates blueberries.

The juice apparently didn't satisfy him, and he kept hanging around my desk or waiting to run into me on my way back from the bathroom. At the end of the day, as he was helping the hair stylists pack up, he came up to my desk and wrote his name and number on a piece of paper, telling me that he did hair and would love to cut mine sometime. What a strange pickup line! But it worked. He was hot, and I really needed to get my hair cut, so I called him. Why not?

A few days later, Justin invited me over to his apartment for a haircut, and it was the first time we really hung out together alone. After the trim, we talked for hours that night. Justin began to randomly call me at work, and if I could, we would chat and get to know each other. It turned out he was from Orange County too, so we started going out in Orange County together and making more and more plans to hang out—though I was smart enough to try to see him without the cameras as much as possible, to give us a real chance to get to know each other. We were always very flirty with each other, and our friends would sometimes comment on our intense connection when we all hung out, though we weren't officially "dating."

When we started to hang out and get to know each other, we became close quickly. We connected over our shared love of music, a closeness with our families, and our goals for the future. Justin was smart, passionate, and able to go deep in conversations with a thoughtful, quiet approach. It was really different and special for a guy at our age to value that kind of connection—especially in LA. We could stay on the phone for five hours straight and never run out of things to say to each other.

I really admired Justin for how he didn't seem to care what other people thought. That enabled him to do his own thing in so many ways, but it also meant he wasn't always in tune with what I was feeling or needing from him. He seemed to think the rest of us were as self-assured and independent as he was. But I wanted to know where we stood, and when I would occasionally ask him if we were together or what we were doing, he would be vague and dismissive. He'd typically respond: "Let's just see what happens. Why do we need a label?"

I still felt sensitive about what other people thought of me—I hadn't developed my thick reality-TV skin yet—and that's ultimately why Justin's natural confidence and self-awareness was so attractive to me.

The only time I saw that confidence waver was when we filmed him cutting my hair for the first season of *The Hills*. We had been hanging out for about two years at this point, and he only agreed very reluctantly. As the production crew set up the lights and mic'ed him in my apartment, I could see him get more and more fidgety. When they were filming, I tried to engage him in conversation, but he got really quiet. Suffice it to say, it wasn't a great scene, and like my hair, it was cut. Justin had been doing my hair since that very first cut in his apartment—even as we started officially dating. My hair was highlighted with blond when I started on *The Hills*, but once Justin started dyeing it, he opted for a dark brown that was almost black. I liked that it felt dramatic, and I liked how much he liked the darker color too. In fact, after we started dating, he ended up doing all of our hair for the first photo shoot for the DVD and promos—and MTV had hired him completely separately on their own. It's funny actually, almost as if our paths would have crossed no matter what.

Because we shared a love of music, we'd often go to shows and check out new punk or rock bands together. Some nights we'd go to the Rainbow Bar on Sunset Boulevard for a drink, then walk down the street to the Viper Room to see who was playing. Sometimes, at his house, we would listen to music for hours, introducing each other to new songs and looking up bands. Justin played the drums in a band of his own, and I'd go watch them practice a lot. And sometimes we went to the beach together and just lay out, soaking in the sunshine. We loved going down to the beach in Newport where our mutual friends lived for big Fourth of July celebrations.

We spent so much time together, and we obviously really liked each other, but we never really talked about "it." Over the years, we've said things to each other about our feelings in the broadest sense, like, "I'll always love you." Or, "I'll always have a special place in my heart for you." But Justin never truly, explicitly said that he loved me. He never opened up in that way.

We took trips together over the next couple of years. We went, just the two of us, to see the Killers in Las Vegas, and we stayed the night at the Hard Rock. We went to Miami and the Bahamas on a big trip with several of my friends. One of my friends, a producer, set up a private jet for a small group of us—which, yes, is just as incredible as it sounds—and I was able to bring Justin along. It was such a fun, relaxed trip, with no drama between Justin and me, particularly because we weren't filming. Hanging out poolside at the Atlantis, he was loving and attentive and friendly as he got to know my friends.

For Christmas in 2008, Justin surprised me with tickets to see Metallica at the Forum in Inglewood. I'd loved Metallica forever, so this was a great gift. We were right down in front, and it was an awesome night. I'll never forget rocking out to "The Unforgiven" with Justin's arms wrapped around my waist. In turn, I surprised him by inviting a bunch of his friends to see one of his favorite bands, Bad Religion, play at the House of Blues in LA.

Concerts aside, Justin's idea of a romantic night out was usually picking me up on his Harley and riding down the Pacific

Coast Highway for an afternoon or sunset drive. I had my own helmet for his bike, and I loved that feeling of sitting behind him, holding on to his chest, with my face pressed against his back. It felt exciting and sexy riding fast down LA streets, in our own bubble as the lights flickered by. Or we'd go to dinner at some cute, dark little spot. Glass of wine, talking in the back booth about life in that profound way you do when you're young and making a deep connection with someone new, getting a little drunk and flirting. We'd walk back to his place and cuddle up for a quiet movie night in. Sometimes we'd get food and go find a spot on the beach, and chill and just talk and enjoy hanging out. Other nights we'd go to one of the little dive bars in Venice by his place and play pool.

Justin and I could hang out, just the two of us, for hours or days, and have so much to talk about. We had intense chemistry from the very beginning, but that developed into an intense, soulful connection over those long conversations. Justin always had such a big heart, and he was always there to listen. I had never met anyone like him. We never got bored of each other.

Of course, it *helped* that our chemistry was off the charts. To this day, I've never had that same spark with anyone else. Sometimes we literally couldn't keep our hands off each other. Justin is a very passionate person, and for him, sex is all about the connection. It's like two souls intertwining, more than a physical act.

That said, the positives also came with negatives, which many fans of *The Hills* are already familiar with. We never specifically talked about being exclusive or in a relationship, but to me, it was just kind of obvious because we were together so much. If I wasn't at his place, he was at mine. We were doing everything together day and night. Maybe I was young and naïve, but in the beginning, before the cameras got involved, it really was great. Justin was showing me that he was much more than just the bad boy or the brooding, mysterious drummer. He was also sensitive and caring, passionate and soulful. It felt like as long as we had each other, we'd be okay. But when he started appearing on the show, everything kind of changed.

After his flop appearance cutting my hair that never made it in the first season, Justin did make it back onto *The Hills*—as you know!—in the third season, because we were still together and hanging out a lot. Viewers were introduced to him as if he had just come into my life, but in reality, we had been dating and spending a lot of time together for a while. He had become someone I confided in, someone from my real life whom I trusted. Once he was on the show, though, we got caught up in the production of it all, like being artificially brought together to film certain scenes, prompted and prodded by production to share a romantic moment or argue about a specific problem. The show could both speed relationships up and pull people apart. Because it's for TV, you push yourself to do things that you normally wouldn't.

Once his episodes began airing, he started seeing what was being said about him—both on the show by me or others, and in the tabloid coverage—and he seemed really annoyed about that. It felt like he was pulling back from me a little, which I understood. In the beginning, he acted like he didn't care what people thought, but when he saw some of his crude behavior and how he came across on-camera, he was definitely upset. In season three, we were (mostly) dating and he was on-camera with me almost every episode. It was clear from the outset that Lauren wasn't his biggest fan, which was—at least in part—a result of the way she saw him treat me. I tried to bring them together in hopes that she could see what I saw in him, but Justin never seemed to cooperate. His worst behavior wasn't just captured on-camera; it always seemed to be in front of Lauren. One night, when I convinced Lauren to join us for drinks, Justin belched loudly at the table, right in our faces. I tried to laugh it off, but I was mortified and uncomfortable. It was pretty gross. The worst was probably the mean things that Lauren and Lo said about him behind our backs when they dished on our relationship. They seemed like catty teenagers giggling as they called him dirty or laughed about his name.

In fact, it was Lo and Lauren who came up with "Justin Bobby" when they couldn't comprehend that his full name is Justin Robert Brescia, and he went by Bobby among his closest friends. So they coined Justin Bobby as a snide nickname. It was so childish and catty, but they kept it up. When he saw it for the first time, it really hurt his feelings.

Even the less malicious comments would bother him. If some of the girls asked me if we were exclusive, or if we'd defined our relationship yet, he would internalize that as pressure to commit or get serious, when I wasn't even the one saying it. If I said something offhand, like, "His toothbrush is upstairs," he would think we were gossiping about him and pull back even more.

I've found that filming makes guys insecure in general. When we were together and there were no interruptions, it was great. After two or three seasons of *The Hills*, I wanted to return to my original goal in LA and start finding TV and movie roles. But as soon as I focused more on my career, and he was doing his own stuff, things got rough. Sometimes he'd be interviewed and say that we were just good friends. The show would push us together more than we really were, but it was still hurtful and confusing when he would disappear for a few days without a word. In response, I would focus elsewhere, on pursuing my acting career, going out with friends, and traveling. I was hardly home on the weekends. He actually brought this up to me recently, saying that it could never really have worked between us because I was so busy. I don't know if I buy that, but he's right that I was concentrating on my career and making important connections.

As part of that focus, I filmed a small role in a movie called *Sorority Row*, a really fun project with an incredible cast, including Rumer Willis, Briana Evigan, and Leah Pipes. A few of my castmates and I were in Las Vegas for the ShoWest Awards where we won the Female Stars of Tomorrow Award and, as usual, having a blast. We were seated at our tables when Rumer kicked me and motioned to something behind me. Before I knew it, Chris Pine was coming up to our table to say hello, and that he'd seen me onstage and thought that I was really beautiful. He asked if he could take me out sometime. I didn't really know who he was, but I did know he was hot. We exchanged numbers, and after he walked away, all of my castmates were so excited.

Shortly after, we went on a date, and Chris picked me up in his cool, old beaten-up car, which I kind of loved. We went to an Italian restaurant that he chose for dinner, and then we went back to his house afterward. He was really into jazz music and loves to read, so he had tons of books filling these huge bookcases. He played the guitar too, and liked to sing, so it seemed I'd found myself another musician. But he didn't like going out and being followed by the paparazzi—he was an introvert, and very focused on his acting. I loved to go out, and of course was usually filming *The Hills*, so our lifestyles were complete opposites in that sense. Still, we tried. We'd go out in Los Feliz or Silver Lake, because the paparazzi were never there. One time a fan did take a picture of us standing next to each other inside a German restaurant. It came out all over the press, and it seemed like he was annoyed. Shortly thereafter I was photographed leaving his house. It started to freak him out.

With my filming schedule, and the fact that there was no way Chris would want to be on the show, I just knew after a couple of months that I couldn't date him. My life was the TV show, and there weren't enough hours in the day to do my job and find time to see him privately. He was a big up-and-coming actor with demands on his time, and it didn't seem like our lives were lining up, even though we really liked each other. We talked and stayed in touch a little after we stopped seeing each other. I have nothing but fond memories of Chris. He was truly one of the most normal people I've ever met in LA—and I mean that as the highest compliment.

Justin was seeing those photos of me and Chris too, and he started getting upset. But we weren't in a committed relationship, and I could go days or even a week without hearing from him. So we broke away from each other a little. He would be out doing what he was doing, and I was dating a little here and there, and we would each get pissed because we still loved each other but he wouldn't commit. There was a lot of hurt involved, and we couldn't seem to break out of the cycle.

Even though there certainly were ups and downs, things were not always what they seemed when it came to my relationship with Justin Bobby. When you watch the show, it seems like I'm obsessed with Justin and feeling every emotion so intensely, while he just broods and says bizarre cryptic things, and then we either break up or move in together. I hope it's clear that there was much more to our relationship. Justin's camera-shyness translated as this calm aloofness on the show. He looked very cool and unemotional most of the time, but I can assure you, when we were alone and off-camera, he was much more romantic—and much clearer about his feelings for me.

Here's an example: we filmed one night at the house I shared with Lauren and Lo, when I lived out back in the pool house. Justin came over with a bottle of wine. The girls weren't home, and we were flirting, drinking wine, and contemplating a swim. Justin was being his usual on-camera self: quiet, saying he didn't want to swim. The producers thought it was getting a little boring, so they asked if I would take my top off in the pool. They offered to cut down on the crew around the pool for privacy, keeping just the bare minimum there. While it was a suggestion or a request, it definitely came with a certain amount of pressure. I agreed to do it, as long as they didn't show anything on-camera. They agreed, and I was filmed only from behind so there was nothing too revealing about the shot. Finally Justin got in the pool. We kissed a little and swam as we talked about an upcoming trip to Cabo. Then they filmed Justin leaving as he said, "See you in Cabo!"

When the episode aired, they'd cut out everything else that happened between Justin and me in the pool, which makes it look like I took my top off and then he left me flat! But in real life, Justin stayed and the production crew left, and we drank our wine and relaxed by the pool before spending the night together.

There were also, unfortunately, some dark moments for us captured on the show, like the night I saw him kiss another girl in front of me. When that happened, it changed something in me. Even though I cried it out and, yes, got back together with him eventually, the trust between us was irrevocably broken. It almost made me feel okay about meeting new guys, going out, or not calling him back. It was a very immature relationship at that point. He was playing games, and, if I'm honest, I was playing games with him back.

We did have periods of being close and spending a lot of time together, and then periods of me feeling betrayed, or Justin playing games, when I would consider us broken up. There was never a huge blowout that resulted in a dramatic breakup, just more frustrations and underhanded comments and confusion. Death by a thousand cuts.

At one point in 2008, Justin and I were in an "off" period when I'd finally had enough of him disappearing for days at a time, or teasing me about dating another guy. I spent the day at the X Games with friends, watching the BMX bike competitions and cheering on a friend, Corey Bohan. I'd met him through a mutual friend, and we'd hung out a few times, casually. The day after his competition, we met up at the pool at the Standard with a bunch of friends. After a fun day of drinking and hanging by the pool, I had to leave to film a scene with Heidi, Spencer, and Justin at this big outdoor concert where Stone Temple Pilots performed. After the scene, it was very clear that Justin thought we were going to hang out for the night, but I left to go back to Corey. We ended up having dinner with all of his friends on the rooftop. The paparazzi captured pictures of us in the pool together and made it look way more romantic than it actually was, which only made it worse.

The next day Justin called me, upset that I was looking so cozy with Corey. I said, "Justin, you won't commit to me, so why should I commit to you? That's not fair." Justin was out there dating and doing God knows what and expected me to be sitting around just waiting for him to call. After years of putting up with it, making excuses, and holding on to hope, I *finally* called him out on the double standard. Years of back and forth, passion and heartbreak, and way too many games were getting to me. I never felt safe with Justin. I always had to protect myself with him and keep my walls up. I finally recognized that my feelings for Justin were holding me back from living my life.

Eventually Justin started not showing up to film when he was supposed to and often ignored calls from producers. He seemed to have his own playbook and his own set of rules, and he just didn't care about anything else. Sometimes he'd just shut his phone off for days. He's that type of person who likes being alone. As frustrating as it can be when he's not reachable, it's also something I loved about him. It became less lovable when he'd disappear on party benders for a week without letting anyone know where he was.

At the end of *The Hills*, Justin and I weren't together. He was on the show because of his relationship with me, and now that we were no longer together, I expected him to go off the air. But he worked with the show to manufacture a relationship with Kristin to keep him in the public eye, which pissed me off.

It's funny to think about how that could only happen before social media. Today, you would see pictures of me on Instagram with a new boyfriend while still acting like Justin and I were together on the show. It could never happen!

I had moved on from Justin and was already dating someone else, but the producers wanted to keep that off-camera and have my continued focus on Justin as a romantic interest. Heidi and Spencer thew a party at their house, and many of us were there filming. I had an event at the Roosevelt to go to afterward, but when I went to leave, the producers wouldn't let me go until I had that confrontation with Kristin over Justin. There really wasn't much for me to say to her. I was finished with Justin and I really didn't care if Kristin and Justin were hanging out—especially because I knew it was just for the show.

Still, production was adamant that we get an explosive scene. So adamant, in fact, that they blocked in my car with production vans and wouldn't let me drive away until I fought with her. I was furious! This was way beyond anything they'd done in the past to get the scene they wanted. I literally couldn't leave. I called my lawyer and my agent, and then my lawyer called the producers to remind them of my legal rights while filming the show. Meanwhile, Kristin didn't want to wait around anymore, so she was there trying to calm me down enough to just film the scene and get it over with. We laughed about it off-camera, but on-camera, we yelled and glared and made it work.

I just wanted to move on, and I felt like Justin was still creating drama for me just so he could remain relevant. It's not like he didn't have a thriving career outside of the show. He still did hair, and his clients included some very well-known names, including Adam Levine. The producers were egging him on and wanted to get that drama however possible. What we wanted really didn't matter.

Meanwhile, Justin's "relationship" with Kristin started out fake, but they began partying together behind the scenes a lot. I think he might have started catching feelings for her, despite his more cynical intentions. I didn't care. I didn't want to know.

I don't think we can look back and say that we ever gave our relationship 100 percent, because of the show. But Justin helped me look at people and situations from a deeper perspective, instead of from the surface. As I think about my future relationships, I know that I would love to find the same passion and intensity I shared with Justin back in the day, just with consistency, safety, and security.

I'm often asked: Will we end up together? For so long, I couldn't answer that question. But the truth is: I cannot say with certainty that our romantic relationship is over. I can't deny our natural connection and chemistry. We've continued to have our ups and downs—like how we ended season one of *The Hills: New Beginnings* on a sour note. Justin was acting very differently on-camera than he was off-camera. Publicly, he was calling me out for telling everyone we kissed and coming on to him, when he was the one flirting and pursuing me. He seemed to be putting his public perception ahead of our real friendship at a time when I needed to lean on him. For the first time ever, I felt so betrayed by him. But we found our way back to talking and rekindling our friendship during the second season of *The Hills: New Beginnings*. I was reminded of how similarly we handle situations and how much we have in common. There were hours filmed of just the two of us hanging out that ended up on the cutting room floor. We spent more time together in the last two years—on- and off-camera—than anyone realizes. In fact, the show filmed an alternate ending for the finale featuring me and Justin holding hands and walking off set, which never aired. I know that we'll continue to be in each other's lives. He was such a big part of my life for so long, and I want to hang on to that. As Justin would say, "Truth and time tell all."

· Chapter Four ·

Playing Audrina

*F*ilming a reality show is a very strange experience, one that certainly shaped me in a lot of ways. I was nineteen when I started, just coming into my own as an adult. I'd just moved to Los Angeles after living nestled among my family in Orange County, and while I wouldn't say that I was sheltered, I definitely still had a lot to learn.

In high school, I was friends with everyone. I had no enemies, no drama. I mean, I was homecoming princess—that should tell you all that you need to know. I received academic awards and social accolades in the yearbook. I wasn't used to drama or mean-girl cattiness, because I never put myself in those situations. My family raised me to be nice to everyone, and that's how I felt it was important to act.

When I started filming *The Hills*, I had to learn how to handle the high school–level gossip and nastiness for the first time. We filmed constantly throughout the year, instead of on a condensed schedule like most other reality shows. And as I've mentioned, the producers constantly prodded for drama. Pretty quickly, the relentless pace and the intrusion by the production crew made the fishbowl experience even more intense.

In some ways, I found all of the production almost therapeutic as I navigated my early twenties, my career, and various relationship issues. On a show, you don't have the option to avoid the person you're having issues with the way you might in real life. Instead, you're forced into a conversation with them, and for the sake of good TV, you dig deep and lay out your grievances. In some ways, it was actually quite healthy, and the producers knew us well enough to ask deep questions and push us toward new conclusions about our relationships or behavior. They were almost like therapists.

On the other hand, sometimes the producers used that personal information to undermine and ambush us to make good TV. They would stoke simmering disagreements and ask pointed questions about our emotional states, sometimes entirely out of the blue, as we walked into filming a new scene. It taught me to be ready for anything, and to this day I'm not afraid of confrontation and know how to handle and express myself in high-pressure situations because of my experience on the show. It was a training ground of sorts. That's what happens when you're prepared to walk into a lion's den 24/7.

While the show groomed me to think on my feet, it also taught me an equally important lesson: to separate myself from my on-screen character. I finally learned this after years of filming, getting hurt, and feeling pushed and manipulated by producers. It's like I was playing a role, while also being myself. On the show, I could share many of my true opinions, thoughts, and feelings, and dictate my hair and wardrobe. But then the producers tell you the storyline for a scene, and you push the conversation in that direction. They specify what they want you to get out of the other person, and you have to improv your way to get there.

Eventually the gray area between what was real and what was produced inspired me to create a separate on-air persona. I could keep my personal life to myself to some degree, and protect myself from being hurt by editing decisions that didn't really reflect me. I could know that it wasn't really me who said something insulting or got insulted; it was "Audrina." Over the course of the first season or two, we began to see that the producers would cut the footage a certain way to manufacture more drama, or they would eliminate a redemptive moment for someone who'd finally spoken her mind. It's no surprise to say that, at a certain point, we stopped trusting most of the producers. I get it; their job is to create dynamic, highly watchable television. I knew we had to meet in the middle to get the job done, but I also had to learn how to protect myself when my feelings got in the way.

They might use voice-overs to put a different spin on a scene in editing, or have another person weigh in on it, which created a whole different level of drama. Or they might simply show someone giving a nasty look from a totally different moment that had nothing to do with the conversation that was actually playing out.

They'd overlay your character with emotions and moods and reactions to craft a more dramatic storyline. It's all real stuff that you said and did, but edited in a very specific way to tell a convenient story.

Still, I almost preferred the fake drama to the editing of more authentic scenes. *That* drove me crazy. There would be lunches or dinners with the girls where I had a lot to say, and I walked away so proud for sticking up for myself or communicating my thoughts clearly during a really emotional, thoughtful conversation. But then in the edited version, they would show me just staring off into the distance and not saying anything. We got a lot of teasing in the press and online for the long, dramatic stares at the ends of scenes, with music in the background. But that wasn't us! It was the editing.

This kind of thing happened often. I would realize a scene or even a particular line I said was cut out to fit a storyline or portray me in a certain way. It just furthered the separation between who I was and the character of "Audrina," and that split was becoming more and more necessary for my sanity.

The voice-over scripts were written by production, and we didn't have a say (pun intended!) in what they wrote to contextualize the scene. They'd show you a small part of the episode, so you could hear the tone of voice, and then you'd read the line a bunch of different ways. These were moments when we expressed our honest feelings and perspectives, but, just like when we filmed a scene, we never knew if what we said would make the final cut. Every Sunday, MTV sent us all DVDs of the episode coming out that week so we could prepare for interviews. I was so excited to watch it, and I got butterflies when I'd open the package because I never knew what to expect.

As a result, some of my family and close friends didn't watch *The Hills*. In the beginning, they would get so mad watching the show and seeing me overreact to something in a way they knew I wouldn't in my personal life, or seeing things I said taken out of context. They saw how I sometimes felt manipulated or guilted into certain scenarios that I would never ever normally put myself in, and they started to get frustrated on my behalf. It became healthier for everyone, not just me, to separate the real Audrina from "Audrina" on TV.

Plus, once my castmates and I entered our early twenties, the addition of alcohol to our social lives introduced a lot of changing social dynamics, new guys and flirtations, and late night arguments after one too many. When you're young and drunk and already used to playing things up a little for the cameras, it's very easy to find yourself in a dramatic moment. At that time, it felt like I had nothing to lose and no real responsibilities, so I went out a lot and had fun.

One of the more bizarre rifts caused by production has to do with the infamous Speidi (as Spencer and Heidi were called) and some fro-yo. I was on my way to meet friends to fly to Las Vegas when Adam DiVello, the producer who found me by the pool, told me to stop by a Pinkberry first for a quick scene. I walked in without really knowing what it was about, and Spencer was there with flowers. It was supposed to look like we were on a romantic little date, but that was not the case. I didn't even know he was going to be there.

After my trip to Vegas, a bunch of us were being filmed on our way into a nightclub. Heidi was working the door at a big event for the public relations firm she worked for, and we were all there to take advantage of the access. Everybody went in, but the producers held me back for a second—and then I saw them hold Spencer back too. Of course this was their plan. Spencer and I then walked in together, separate from the group, so it looked like we showed up together. As ridiculous as it sounds, Heidi really thought I was into him and trying to make moves on her man. She was genuinely upset. That's what started a little feud between me and Heidi for a while, where she was talking shit about me. And all it took was two small, seemingly harmless things: staging a fro-yo encounter, and holding us both back for a minute at the club.

I couldn't believe that Heidi was taking the "connection" between me and Spencer to heart, when I had assured her there was nothing going on on- or off-camera. They were always so serious about each other, and I never would have gotten in the middle of that relationship, but she didn't believe me—and then she began taking it out on me. I went to her birthday party shortly after the Vegas trip with the hopes of wishing her a happy birthday and burying the hatchet. She was so rude to me, even as I was trying to smooth things over. Some of her other friends who were there piled on, calling me names and telling me I should just leave. I remember that was the first time I ever cried on-camera, because I couldn't believe how mean they were. I'd never been treated that way in my life.

It was the beginning of a lesson that was really hard to learn. My castmates were my friends, but they weren't always people I could confide in or trust. It was really tough, especially when I was going through some difficult times and wanted to open up to and lean on them. But they taught me, over and over, where they stood. They were just my TV friends.

Not only were things often staged, but editing could sometimes change entire events. I had a birthday party at the London Hotel on the rooftop with all of my friends, and my brother was there, and the show was, of course, filming it. The crazy thing was that it was edited to look like Heidi and Spencer's engagement party, complete with a toast from Spencer. The producers knew how they were framing the party and prompted Spencer to make it look like he was hosting.

Kristin arrived at that same event, and I was glad to see her. We hung out occasionally off-camera. Kristin was dating one of Justin's friends when I was with Justin, so we'd all get together from time to time. I was so excited about her coming on the show. But apparently Kristin came ready to heat things up. When I approached her to hash it out over Justin, we got into a fiery argument. The thing is that Kristin is a very smart businesswoman, and she was hired onto *The Hills* to be the bitch. She had to stir up drama and "tell it like it is." So she saw an opportunity to create some drama with me over Justin, and she went for it. I get it!

Another savvy reality TV vet is Stephanie Pratt, the queen of stirring the pot. Stephanie doesn't actually have a lot to say on her own, but she wanders around looking for opportunities to create drama between friends. And that's what she did at this party. She went back and forth between me and Kristin, telling me what Kristin was allegedly saying behind my back, and then telling Kristin how mad I was. They both knew their roles and played them well.

The difference between Kristin and Stephanie is that Stephanie truly is a troublemaker. That's who she's always been, both on-camera and off. I'd been warned for years to be careful around her, and never to trust her. I've been told that she's not loyal. She's not there for you. She turns her back on you in a second. And my experiences with her to come, on *The Hills: New Beginnings*, would prove it.

Developing the thick skin meant that if the tabloids, or random bloggers, or strangers said mean things about me, I could let it roll off my shoulders. But it didn't protect me when someone I thought I was close to, someone I valued and trusted, spoke badly about me.

The show gave us a strange opportunity to see what our friends were saying about us behind our backs. And the truth is: it can be really hurtful, even if I know they are amping it up for the camera. Sometimes even the small comments can surprisingly sting. Like when we went on a big group trip to Costa Rica. While I was loving our time away at the beautiful beaches, it didn't come without its drama. We were having some fun girl moments, dancing at the outdoor nightclub and taking turns making different mixed drinks. The crew was Kristin, Stephanie, me, and Stacie the Bartender, who'd made a couple of earlier appearances but came around more when Kristin joined the show. At that time, I was dating Ryan Cabrera off-camera and nobody knew because the producers wanted me to keep the Justin thing going on-camera. And when I watched the episode, Stacie made some really nasty comments in a conversation with Kristin, including calling me a "Stage 5 clinger" with Justin. It was so rude, and she didn't even know the whole story!

That was the lesson I was learning the more I filmed: no one would really ever know the true story, so instead of fighting the inevitable, it was better to play the part and just enjoy the ride.

In a lot of ways, the toughening up I had to do to deal with the pressures and editing within the show helped me to deal with the spotlight and attention I was receiving *because* of the show. Almost straight out of high school, I was thrown into the lion's den with bloggers like Perez Hilton calling me all sorts of names, body shaming me, making fun of everything about me. It was overwhelming. All of those little comments slowly tear at you. It all gets in your head. Just as I learned to protect myself by playing "Audrina," I also developed these walls to guard against everyone and everything. I got to the point where anyone could say mean things to my face and I wouldn't feel hurt anymore—which is not a natural or good thing, in hindsight.

There was pressure to be so many different things at a time when I was still trying to figure out who I was. I was in my early twenties and I was getting offered fantastic opportunities that I knew so many girls would kill for. I recognize the incredible position I was in. But still, I had to decide who I wanted to be. For a while, I asked everyone in my life—agents, managers, publicists, friends, family—what I should do. I worried too much about what other people thought—whether they liked me or respected me. It's classic LA, but classic reality TV too: you're constantly worried about what everyone else thinks about you and your work. It's an energy-consuming and time-consuming tug-of-war.

I finally tuned back into what I wanted when I was offered to do the cover of *Playboy*. My agent and my whole team thought it was a great idea. I was told I'd be working with one of the best photographers, and it would be tasteful (sexy but covered up). I had to ask myself: Was *Playboy* the direction I wanted to go in? The answer was no. I just didn't want to do it. I might have considered it when I was younger and modeling regularly, but at that point, I knew it wasn't the type of career that I wanted to build. I had my success, and now I wanted to be mindful about how I was establishing my name and image. I kept thinking about what my grandparents, or my cousins, would think if they saw it. Plus, I was already getting a lot of backlash for my relationships on the show. I'd learned the hard way how difficult it is to navigate backlash like that. I didn't want to give anyone anything else to attack me for, especially if I wasn't passionate about what I was doing. Some things are worth the drama. *Playboy* wasn't.

I was learning to walk the line of being provocative and flirty without being overly sexualized. I was known as the "bikini queen" and I wasn't shy about posing in a bathing suit or lingerie. I agreed to do a few photo shoots for the popular magazines *Maxim* and *FHM*. Yes, they were pretty sexy photos, but I felt like these were more pop culture–based publications with a younger, hipper vibe.

I got to do some really fun small roles in movies like *Into the Blue 2* and the thriller *Sorority Row*, but I also turned down opportunities that seemed too sexualized, like playing a stripper or other roles like that. I just wasn't interested in taking my career in that direction. Looking back, I'm still proud of the backbone I showed in saying no to the opportunities I felt strongly about. But I also could have taken a more mature approach and tried to turn those opportunities into something I *was* comfortable with. I could have said that I was willing to do the role with certain suggestions and changes. Or asked, at least, to discuss with the director or producer why the character was making certain choices or if they could be dialed back. Now I can see my agent's side more clearly: certain things would have been good opportunities. But they just felt like the complete opposite of who I was. I guess that's acting, though, right?

Still, I have no regrets. Standing up for myself then was an important lesson that I'm trying to relearn today. I want to harness more of that bold, outspoken girl I was back then.

· *Chapter Five* ·

Round and Round We Go

I first met Corey in 2006 through a good friend named Angela. Back when we met, I had been trying to move on from Justin Bobby after years of a hot-and-cold relationship. It seems like I was always trying to move on from Justin back then! One night, Angela called and encouraged me to put my Justin troubles aside for the night: "Screw Justin. I'm coming to pick you up right now! I'm taking you to a party at my friend's house. He's a BMX rider and he has the hottest friends!" I figured, *Why not, what have I got to lose?* I welcomed a distraction from Justin, something—or someone—to get my mind off of him.

So Angela picked me up and we drove out to the party seemingly in the middle of nowhere, almost two hours outside of LA. It turns out her friend who was having the party was Corey Bohan, and it was at his house. It was a quintessential bachelor

pad that he shared with two roommates. It was clean and organized, which I'd come to learn was his style. The bar was fully
stocked. There must have been dozens of bottles of Jack Daniel's
on display.

We walked in and surveyed the scene: lots of hot guys mill-
ing around, clearly letting loose, and lots of pretty girls. People
were gathered in the kitchen making drinks and playing drinking games in the living room. Corey had just placed first in the
X Games, and he was clearly going all-out in celebration. Angela
introduced me to him and his girlfriend when we arrived, and
right off the bat, I could detect his magnetism and charm.
Even though I noticed he was cute, it wasn't a love-at-first-sight
moment. There wasn't an instant connection or any sign of what
was to come, which was a good thing because he had his girlfriend
on his arm. The party didn't disappoint; it was full of professional
athletes blowing off steam after a huge competition. Angela was
right: a night of hanging out in the testosterone-filled BMX world
was just what I needed to take my mind off Justin.

Angela started inviting me to hang out with these guys more
often, and she'd set up fun group activities in Orange County or
up in LA, like big dinners, or bowling, or meeting up at a bar. For
Halloween, we all went to this haunted house downtown. Angela
became our friend group's de facto social director. Corey was part
of the group, but he wasn't always there—he'd pop in and out. I
was always glad to see him, but again, it's not like there were any
sparks happening. We were just in the same group, all hanging
out together.

At some point, maybe a year or two later, Corey must have broken up with his girlfriend, because he sent me a message on Myspace. (Yes, I'm definitely dating myself here, but Myspace was the place to be back in 2008.) When I didn't respond to the first messages, he kept writing to let me know when he would be in LA next or suggest we hang out. I didn't think much of it, because in his messages he was always inviting me out as part of group hangs, never a proper date. Besides, I was still on and off with Justin, and between that and filming *The Hills*, my plate was full.

The following Halloween, a whole two years after Corey and I first met, Lauren and I were throwing a big Halloween party, which you might remember from the show. She suggested we try to up our game and invite some new guys into the mix. We racked our brains for some new (preferably good-looking) friends, and I naturally thought of Corey's group of BMX athletes. I'd just confronted Justin after catching him kissing another girl (what I wish I could tell my younger self . . .), so I was definitely ready to meet new people and do some flirting. So we included them, along with our whole group, including Whitney, Brody, and our friend Frankie Delgado, who'd also joined the show. My brother, Mark, and sister Casey came too. We really did it up that night, with spooky decorations and a fog machine. I dressed as Madonna—a classic, and not too slutty—and Lauren dressed up as a flapper. I remember Corey wore a full white sailor suit, which looked adorable on his six-foot frame. He texted me that he was on his way, and I felt butterflies as the camera crew lined up by the door to capture the moment. It was kind of a big deal to bring a new guy into the mix, and I still didn't really know if I was interested, or if he was interested. Luckily, he fit right in and everyone seemed to like him right off the bat.

And that was Corey's debut on *The Hills*. The producers wanted to capture me hanging out with a new guy, to give Justin a run for his money on-air. Apparently they sensed some good chemistry between us—or they just really wanted to create some drama with Justin—because shortly after, they asked me to film a date with Corey. I had to call him and basically ask him out and see if he'd be willing for them to film us having dinner together.

Corey agreed to the setup, so we went out for sushi at a restaurant called Katana, and that's when I really saw him for the first time. He was definitely nervous in front of the cameras, and who could blame him? Our first date was filmed! Still, he was attentive and asked me questions, and after dealing with Justin's silly games for so long, it felt kind of nice just to be out and talking with someone new. At this point, now that I knew he was interested and that I might be too, there were definitely a few sparks flying. The thing I remember most was how I felt with Corey, which was such a stark contrast to how I felt with Justin or a few other guys I'd been on dates with. He was a gentleman, and he treated me really well on dates, always opening doors and pulling my chair out, asking me what I wanted and sometimes ordering for both of us, and he often picked up the bill. I felt taken care of, secure, safe. It was a nice change of pace.

We kissed that first night, off-camera. Corey dropped me off at my apartment—the one I shared with Lauren—and before I got out of his car, he leaned in for a kiss. It was passionate and lingering, but what I remember most wasn't the kiss itself but the way he looked at me afterward, like he was studying my face and really saw me. Damn! Now there was a *definite* spark.

Up until that point, I'd thought of the date as just a setup for the show. You can have fun flirting with someone on-camera, but once the crew packs up, so often those sparks are gone until the next time someone calls "action." But that kiss was off-camera, which meant that Corey really felt something for me. He was definitely growing on me, but with Justin still partially in the picture, I just wasn't sure. Still, it was worth seeing if there was anything there. We went on a few more dates, which went just as well as the first, all things considered. Corey was still new in front of the cameras, and it takes most people a while to get rid of those nerves and jitters—never mind being on a date with someone you're still trying to feel out.

It soon became clear that the producers were encouraging me to spend more time with Corey to try to bait Justin. Corey seemed like such a good, stand-up guy, and I didn't want to hurt him by making him a pawn of the show. The producers were right, though: whether I liked it or not, Corey was making Justin jealous. On-camera, Justin acted like he didn't care, but he was actually getting pretty upset off-camera. He would see a paparazzi photo of Corey and me out to dinner, and even if I hadn't heard from Justin in a week or two, he would immediately call me. In his broody way, he would probe for details and add in his sarcastic opinion, which I saw as a way of showing jealousy while playing it cool. But Justin wasn't sitting home pining away for me. He was out dating too. It was such a double standard and so emotionally manipulative, which I told him.

Corey was fun and lighthearted, and never seemed to play games about texting or calling me back or making plans. One night, he and I went out wearing these ridiculous wigs because we wanted to meet our friends out at a bar in Hermosa Beach without being recognized. We were total goofballs together and it felt really good. Of course, we ended up running into Justin at the bar, who handled it exactly as immaturely as you would imagine. He kept antagonizing Corey by looking over at me and winking. And then Justin texted me something along the lines of: "Just know that you're mine, first and always." Unfortunately, Corey saw that text, which caused this huge fight between us. With Justin, he wants me or he doesn't want me, but either way, no one else can have me.

Corey and I were definitely feeling each other out, but it didn't seem like it needed to be *too* serious. We stayed in touch, and we'd try to see each other whenever he was in town, which wasn't often due to his travel schedule. If he was home, we'd meet up at the same bar with our friends. You know how it is to be twenty-three, when every night out is with your group of friends and you're meeting up and flirting with different people. If we were together in a big group, he would find ways to stand next to me or tend to me throughout the night. Even so, he was dating other girls, which was fine with me because I was dating other guys or talking to Justin. Corey and I had a connection, and we liked each other on some level, but the stars weren't aligned for us to act on it.

Gradually, as I spent time with Corey, I learned a lot more about him. He shared details of his past relationships and what he was looking for, his hopes for the future. He asked me a lot of questions and showed a genuine interest in my life, always wanting to know what I'd done over the weekend or who I was out with the night before. Everything with Justin was more guarded, full of innuendo and nuance, and I hated that I was attracted to his veiled, flirtatious way of speaking. I could already see the appeal of such a strong, straightforward guy. I felt a little lighter, a little happier, with him.

We weren't dating seriously, but we'd been seeing each other often enough that when Lauren and our group went to a beautiful Malibu house party that we filmed for the show, I invited Corey to come along. It was a beautiful day spent floating around a gorgeous pool with great food and drinks. It felt so good to be with him and my friends, not to have to play games and deal with sarcastic remarks meant to hurt or confuse. It made all the sense in the world for me to focus on him and leave Justin for good.

After my epiphany at that Malibu party, Corey was in and out of town a lot, and it was hard to make plans for a while. I was going with the flow and not putting too much pressure on forcing a relationship with him while he was traveling, which meant that I started talking to Justin *again*. I felt that magnetic pull to Justin so strongly, even though part of me was still thinking about Corey.

Whether or not I wanted to see Justin didn't matter. He was on the show, and he was going to be a part of my life no matter what. In real life, it would have been much easier to break things off with Justin and take some time apart, but not in this situation. Plus, my relationship with Justin had started as a deep friendship, and it was really hard to cut him off. I wanted to hold on to that friendship and trust. At the same time, Justin had never wanted to commit to me 100 percent, so I didn't feel like I owed him an explanation of anyone I was dating. He certainly didn't provide explanations to me when he was out with other women. Corey and I were just barely starting to get to know each other, and we kept it very casual while he traveled, with no promises made. So, as confusing as it felt to me at the time, I didn't have any moral qualms.

My energy was so confusing that *The Hills'* production team asked me what was going on. I was clearly talking to Justin a lot. The producer said, "If you're getting back together with Justin and breaking up with Corey, let us know! We need to film it!" It was strange to have that outside pressure. I wasn't breaking up with Corey because we weren't really together. And I wasn't getting back with Justin because we were never officially together. Couldn't a girl date in peace?

I look back on this time now and see a young woman worrying so much about other people's feelings instead of taking the time to explore her options and get to know what she wanted in a relationship. I never put myself first. If I got into a tense situation with someone, I always worried about what they were going to feel. I never cared about how *I* would feel. It's not a way that I would ever want to live again.

To appease the producers, I filmed a date with Corey and basically let him know the truth that my heart was still with Justin. It just didn't feel fair to lead him on, and I certainly didn't want to bring him onto the show knowing it would cause an issue with Justin. Corey wasn't experienced with reality television and the manipulated drama that goes along with it. I genuinely cared about him, and I didn't want to put him through that. I knew I had to fully close this door with Corey before I could give someone else all of my attention. That was the last time Corey filmed with me on *The Hills*. As you know, I kept seeing Justin, for better or for worse. Mostly worse.

Justin and I continued to see each other off-camera for a while longer. It looked worse on the show than it felt in private. But he still would disappear here and there, and I would hear about him with other girls, until it was finally enough.

After Justin and I really ended it, toward the end of filming *The Hills*, I started dating the musician Ryan Cabrera. Ryan and I had been close friends for years and years. When I was eighteen, before I even moved to LA, I worked at a music label in Newport Beach and met him through a mutual friend there. One night my friend and I went to Forty Deuce in LA. I was a few years away from twenty-one, but not only did I get in, I soon found myself dancing onstage with the club's dancers. Ryan was there with a group of friends from the music label. And over too many drinks, I got to know him a little. He was so much fun and so high-energy, we just laughed and danced with our friends all night.

We became fast friends, and I was soon on the go-to invite list for his infamous house parties. Ryan would invite us to all of his events and parties and comedy shows in LA, and we ran into each other out all the time. So over the next several years we built up a close friendship. Ryan got to know my siblings and is friends with my brother to this day.

Ryan is truly the happiest person on earth, and such a delight to be around. Over time, we felt like there were sparks. There was no big discussion of should we or shouldn't we. It just happened so naturally, even while the core of our friendship stayed the same. Ryan planned romantic and fun activities for us, including a particularly lovely weekend in New York. We were just always with each other, and then he started staying at my house. We exercised and hiked together, and Ryan was always looking for a cool show to check out or a fun party to hit, so we were out and living it up in our twenties.

The thing about Ryan is that he's so nice, so giving, and so loving. He was always up for anything, planning a social event, or traveling somewhere. His schedule was full, and his energy was apparent. Sometimes I felt like his lifestyle of always doing *everything* was just a lot. When you're close friends with someone and then start dating, the relationship automatically starts from a pretty intense place. We skipped the getting-to-know-each-other phase and launched right into something more real. In fact, Ryan lived with me for a few months after he sold his house and was still hunting for a new place, so the emotional intensity was compounded by spending almost every second together. At the same time, the producers wanted me to spend more time with him on-camera, to really establish our relationship on the show. Ryan was happy to do it, and I was glad to be with someone who obviously felt so strongly about me and wasn't afraid to show it. But I admit, I felt a little stifled.

When you bring someone onto a show to film, the dynamics of your relationship change, no matter how hard you fight against it. Producers want certain things from you both, and that makes you start to question what feelings are performative and which are real. And I think that was happening a little for me and Ryan as the producers wanted us to film more and more.

Compared to Justin, Ryan was emotionally available and there for me no matter what. He would show up and surprise me with my favorite candy, or trips, or anything to brighten my day. He was always thoughtful and kind, and so romantic. He'd cook dinner for me with music and candlelight, or set up a movie night outside with blankets. I was truly not used to this type of consistency and attention. With Justin there was a lot more uncertainty, days or weeks of no communication, and constant wondering where I stood. The flip side of that was space and independence. I was used to doing what I wanted to do and having time to myself when he disappeared for a few days. I know it sounds crazy to say that Ryan was too present, but that's what it felt like in my twenty-five-year-old head.

On the occasions he wasn't around, things were difficult for a different reason. Ryan is also a pop star and touring musician with a big, loyal following, and when he traveled to play shows,

I would hear that he was maybe talking to other women. That hurt, especially when so much of my time with Justin had been spent questioning his loyalty. Ryan was so available to me when we were together in LA, but I didn't want to have to deal with the uncertainty when he traveled.

I loved Ryan's personality and spending time with him, but at the end of the day, I was torn. He truly is such a great guy, yet I couldn't shake the feeling that it wasn't right, that I wasn't as head-over-heels as I wanted to be. Above all, I never wanted to hurt him or jeopardize our friendship. It was hard to tell him that I thought we were better off as friends, but I didn't want to let things fester to the point where we hated each other and never wanted to talk again.

Thankfully, Ryan took it well, and we have been friends ever since. Well, except for that time a couple years ago when we temporarily got back together. What can I say? I don't let many people into my heart, so once I do, it's easy to give them another chance.

And miraculously, we're *still* friends even after a second breakup. We talk regularly, and as of this writing he's engaged. I'm so happy for him that he found his person! We've always cared about each other, and we always will.

Unfortunately, even though I'd broken up with Ryan off-camera, that didn't quite fit the narrative of the show. I was scheduled to watch him perform at the iHeartRadio Wango Tango music festival; it was already on the production schedule as a group event, and the producers wanted me to film the scene anyway. So, a few days after I'd broken up with Ryan, I had to film watching him perform. What can I say, it makes good TV. When we were done, I left and drove to my parents' house crying. And it just so happened that Corey called me while I was driving, because he had just gotten back in town.

What happened next proves the saying "timing is everything." And one thing Corey has above all else is incredible timing.

· *Chapter Six* ·

All Good Things Must Come to an End

*A*fter six high-octane seasons of *The Hills*, it was over. To celebrate, MTV threw a huge, televised finale party at the Roosevelt
Hotel in Hollywood for the whole cast and crew. It was a celebration of our incredible run and a look back at all of the fun we'd
had over the last four years. Everyone was there, including Justin,
Kristin, Brody, Lo, and even Lauren, who came back to join us for
the occasion. While the final episode aired in July 2010, we had
actually stopped filming a few weeks before, and it was incredible how much I already missed seeing everyone every day. After
all, I'd spent countless hours with them, most days per week,
for the last several years. As part of the event, MTV also showed
video clips from over the years, and we each had a chance to look
back and reminisce about the fun (and sometimes embarrassing)
moments. It was a big production, and I'm so glad we got to cel-

ebrate more privately with an after party at Teddy's, a restaurant at the Roosevelt, just for cast and crew, family and friends. There were no cameras allowed. Just lots of champagne toasts, hugs and tears, and rehashing of stories from the last few years. It had been such a hugely meaningful journey for all of us.

I brought Corey to that finale party as my date. We had just rekindled our relationship a month or two prior, not long after I'd ended things with Ryan. And we had such a fun night. We danced and laughed, and he was such an easy, outgoing date—somebody who was there to have a good time but was also emotionally supportive of me during such a huge moment and career milestone.

The first week off from filming felt really nice, the way I usually felt whenever I had scheduled time off from production. But by the time I got to weeks two and three without filming, it began to sink in. For the first time in almost five years, I didn't have a production schedule to follow or a small crew following me around, checking my mic and asking me to repeat a conversation so they could film it with different lighting. I was so used to being told what to do every day—where to be, what to talk about—that being alone was truly a shock to my system. Over the course of those years, my crew members and production team had really started to feel like family. Now I was on my own, for better or for worse.

Before that point, it hadn't quite hit me that I had to figure out what I was going to do next. I had to create a completely new lifestyle and a new routine, decide what *I* wanted to do and where *I* wanted to go. It sounds a little crazy, honestly, but so much of my time was at MTV's discretion that I had to relearn how to make my own choices about my time and live on my own terms.

The Hills wrap party was a bit of a coming out for me and Corey as a couple, and I felt ready to give him a real chance now that I'd had time to move on from Justin. I ignored Justin at the wrap party, even though I felt him looking at Corey and me. Finally things were clicking for us: after a few hits and misses, Corey and I were officially dating, and I was feeling the happiness that I deserved. We'd go to big dinners or nights out with our friends, or to the movies or bowling or karaoke. He was always up for a good time, and he always made me laugh.

Without as many obligations in LA, I started going back to Orange County more often to see my family. It was nice to be able to really hang out there and relax, without rushing to drive back to LA as soon as we finished dinner. I was spending more time with Corey and focusing on our relationship. I wasn't going out as much either. It was different, but it all felt really good, like I was settling into something calmer, less hectic, more grounded. It was refreshing.

So refreshing, in fact, that I intended to take some real time off. I imagined myself holed up in a little house on the beach, away from the hustle and drama of the city and the long lenses of the paparazzi. I felt like I needed to take a deep breath after years of constant filming, parties, and events. I wanted to step away from the reality TV grind and think about what I really wanted for myself.

When Corey went with me to an awards show that year, that was the moment our relationship really solidified. Having our picture in the tabloids and walking arm in arm down the red carpet made it official. It's kind of funny when you think about it: ultimately, we didn't make the decision for ourselves. We just followed the lead of the paparazzi.

Early on, Corey was never shy about PDAs and making it known that we were together, even on trips to Vegas or Mexico where paparazzi followed us. He seemed so proud to have me as his girlfriend, especially in front of his friends.

We really got to know each other, and it brought us even closer together. He told me how he left Australia when he was young to pursue his dream of BMX racing. I can't imagine being so far away from my family for so long. It really tugged at my heartstrings.

As an athlete, he was so responsible, always taking his career and business opportunities seriously and professionally. He woke up early, worked out, played golf and tennis, and took such good care of himself. At that point, he was so focused on his health and career that partying wasn't an option. That was such a breath of fresh air to me. There were never late nights of one-too-many with the guys, daylong hangovers, drunk dials, or shady girls hanging around. I was so attracted to his healthy lifestyle, the way he seemed more mature than guys getting wasted at clubs and parties late into the night.

Corey loved to cook for me and would sometimes make me a delicious steak or salmon dinner, complete with candlelight and wine. He was incredibly sweet and charming, and never short on compliments. He always said that I had the biggest heart and was so kind; he liked the fact that everyone liked me; and he told me how beautiful I was. He was very sweet.

We spent so many days at the beach, just the two of us. He would surf, I would lie out, and we'd get lunch and eat at the park nearby. Those were the days I felt most at peace. During our quiet beach days together, I would open up about the pressures I was feeling about filming or career decisions, and he would give me advice. He'd talk me through the possible outcomes of whatever I was dealing with in a way that made the situation feel so much easier to handle. I was learning to leave the drama on the show.

In the beginning, Corey was so romantic. Once for Valentine's Day, he booked a room at the Surf and Sand Resort in Laguna Beach, which had rose petals on the bed when we arrived, and planned a romantic dinner for us. He gave me the nicest card, pouring his heart out. He was always able to share his feelings for me—good or bad.

We were young, without real responsibilities, and I loved to be spontaneous. I would realize we didn't have commitments for a few days and suggest we get out of town. We'd buy tickets to Cabo and just go. Once, I woke up in LA and saw that it was raining outside, which meant it was snowing in Big Bear. I suggested we drive up there and get a cabin for a day or two. And off we'd go. Corey was more of a planner than I was, and sometimes he'd take a little convincing, but we would always go.

He pushed me out of my comfort zone, and I pushed him out of his. I helped him to be spontaneous, and he helped me find more courage at times to do things that scared me and to be myself. It's pretty ironic to think about that now.

Plus, no one messed with me when I was with Corey. At six feet tall with a very athletic build, he always made me feel protected. If there was ever an issue with someone at a club—you know how some late nights out can go in your twenties, right?—he was always there, stepping in front of me to defuse and protect. You'd be surprised how often drama starts when you're being filmed for a TV show or followed by paparazzi. Random people inside the bar or club could get aggressive and mean. Girls especially would yell stuff at us, or sometimes throw ice. Once, someone threw a glass at Lauren's head when we were sitting at a back table in a club. It was terrifying! That's why we always went out in groups. With Corey, I felt safe and cared for. I didn't have to constantly watch my back because he always had my back. It felt really nice to finally let my guard down.

Corey would talk up some of the things I was doing professionally to his friends. I even sometimes heard him on the phone with his family back in Australia proudly sharing my accomplishments. Sometimes I found it hard to tell if he was into me because of my personality or because I was famous. He liked the free stuff that brands or companies would send me, and the free vacations that we'd bring his friends or family on. I loved having family and friends around, so I was very open to his mom and dad coming on a trip to Bali with us, or inviting his friends on other trips. But then he started getting more and more annoyed when my work commitments took my time and attention, or when I was recognized when we were out together.

If I'd really been paying attention, I would have seen the warning signs. There's a fine line between being affectionate and proud and being possessive and jealous. When Corey and I were out, he would put his arm around me and pull me close if he sensed another guy getting ready to talk to me, or frankly even coming close to me. I'm friendly, and I know a lot of people out in LA. When our relationship was still fresh, I didn't see that as an act of jealousy. Instead, I felt proud that he wasn't afraid to show everyone that he cared about me. When he wanted to know what guy friends I was talking to, or didn't want me to hang out with them, I liked it. It was kind of cute that he cared like that. After all, Justin was never that physically affectionate.

Then Corey's insecurity took center stage.

Two months after we rekindled, I began rehearsing for season eleven of *Dancing with the Stars* in September 2010. The show was (and is) huge, with a monster viewership and so much attention. Coming off *The Hills*, I thought this was a great way to show the world another side of my personality. It would be part of my transition from MTV reality star to hostess and actress. Everyone knows that training and practicing for *DWTS* is grueling, but I was determined to put in the work and do well. It was a huge opportunity—plus, I love music and dancing. I was so excited!

My partner was Tony Dovolani, a truly wonderful, supportive teacher. I was so afraid to get a partner who was tough and mean and bossy, so being paired with Tony was a relief. We got along well, but he was also hard on me when he needed to be, pushing me to my limits and giving me constructive feedback.

The rehearsal hours were long, which I often made longer by insisting that we not stop until I nailed it. Of course, the longer we rehearsed, the more exhausted my body and brain became. I remember a lot of moments where I would just keep falling or stumbling, and Tony would say, "Enough, Audrina. Go home for the night."

The brightest spot of the whole experience was meeting the other competitors, including Michael Bolton, Florence Henderson, Brandy, Bristol Palin, and Jennifer Grey. I love the movie *Dirty Dancing*, so I was over the moon to meet Jennifer. We had a chance to hang out backstage during dress rehearsals, and it was such an interesting mix of people.

The entire experience was like stepping out of my own world and entering that of the professional dancers. The season's cast and I were brought into their inner sanctum, invited to join them at their favorite Russian spa to recover after grueling rehearsals. We would all get massages, sit in the sauna, or relax with some tea. The professional dancers, including Derek Hough, Maksim Chmerkovskiy, Cheryl Burke, and Karina Smirnoff, were a tight-knit family, and they brought us all under their wings during the season. Tony invited me along to real professional dance competitions, where we saw nationally renowned dancers show their stuff. It was so inspiring to see the individual styles and the artistry they brought to the dance floor, not to mention the costumes. I also watched YouTube videos of professional competitions, and really immersed myself in dance.

The professional dancers would always look out for all of us, giving us pointers or tips throughout the week when they saw us. For instance, when Maksim saw me sitting in a strange position during a break from rehearsals, he made sure to correct me so I didn't overstretch a tired muscle. They all kind of watched out for us. That's not to say the competition wasn't fierce. It was an interesting combination of camaraderie and wanting to win. We would get some people sneaking peeks of their competitors' dress rehearsals to see what they were up against. I remember Brandy and Jennifer Grey, who ultimately won, were both very serious and in the zone whenever we went to dress rehearsals the day before our live dances.

The intensity of *DWTS* distracted me from my relationship with Corey. We were spending less time together, and I wasn't returning texts or calls as quickly as usual because I put my phone away while I was rehearsing. Soon, he accused me of sleeping with Tony. Tony is a happily married man with three beautiful kids. He's a real family man—period, full stop. There wasn't even a hint of anything inappropriate! But Corey wouldn't let it go. Every single day, he would make rude, nasty comments about Tony and what he was so sure was going on. Corey accused me of making the dances too sexy and inappropriate, as if I had control over the steps of the tango. Whenever I was home, he was always in my face, questioning me and insinuating that Tony was getting handsy, or that our dancing had evolved into something sexual.

When I wasn't home, he was constantly calling or texting to keep tabs on me. Corey was busy with his career, training and traveling for competitions or doing sponsorship work for Red Bull—yet he still had the time and energy to obsess about what I was doing all the time. Of course, the paparazzi coverage might have contributed.

Frankly, I was embarrassed. I knew that Tony and some other people on the show were starting to notice—the stress was clearly affecting my headspace in rehearsals—and I didn't want them to get the wrong impression of me, or of Corey. The accusations also made me take a step back to consider, *Is this wrong? Am I being too touchy?* He started to get in my head and make me question myself. Corey would come to the live performances and eliminations on Mondays or Tuesdays to watch me perform. He acted so loving and proud of me in front of the cameras and the other dancers, before blowing up and yelling at me once we got home.

My experience on *DWTS* was intense. With Corey in my head, and my perfectionist tendencies, I worked hard and was starting to break down by the end of my run. Performing onstage in front of millions of people watching at home was exciting and very nerve-racking. I would get butterflies and a little shaky before each dance, especially for my very first one. Tony and I were up first, performing the very first dance of the whole season. I remember standing on the stage, and after practicing to the studio recording of our song, "California Gurls" by Katy Perry, I wasn't prepared for the show's live band to perform it. I wasn't able to find the exact cue I'd been trained to start on, so with my heart beating out of my chest, I had to improv. I stood there with my back to the audience and began to shake my hips and raise my arms in the air to buy a few seconds until I found the right beat to begin. It looked intentional, and I got on the beat to start our dance, just glad to get through it. Tony always had my back on the dance floor. He could look into my eyes and calm my nerves. And when I missed a step or lost the count, he would know just what to do to get us back on track, sometimes physically moving me into place, or spinning me out and back in to recover. What-ever he did, I always felt like I had a safety net and we pulled it off. The judges—Len Goodman, Bruno Tonioli, and Carrie Ann Inaba—didn't pull any punches either when they were critiquing our performances.

It's funny how little control we had over the creative aspects of our performance. We had some input into the costumes, but we didn't pick the music or have the final say. The show asks each of the competitors to list some of their favorite songs to see if they might work for one of our dances, and sure enough, none of mine were selected for me. All's fair in reality TV, I guess. For the most part I was fine with the music, except when they selected *The Hills* theme song "Unwritten" by Natasha Bedingfield for the rumba, which felt like a very weird fit for such a sensual dance. In fact, that was the one time I was uncomfortable with the performance. The rumba is a very sexy dance, which I didn't realize, and the choreography brought Tony and me together the closest physically. There was a lot more writhing around than I was used to. When I watch it back, I can see that I'm uncomfortable when doing it. It was all a performance, and we were both professionals, but I wasn't used to being so up close and personal with someone.

One of my favorite parts of *DWTS* was the costumes and stepping into my role as a professional dancer. The show's costume designer was terrific and I was able to make small suggestions here and there, while leaving a lot of it up to Tony, who knew best. I felt like I was cast as "the sexy one" on the show, which meant that my costumes were even more fun to play with. I was a professional and I could certainly "play Audrina."

I was eliminated in week six at the end of October, and I was truthfully surprised. It never seemed like we had the lowest scores, and, in fact, we had the second-highest score that week. Truthfully, I breathed a sigh of relief that I didn't have to continue under Corey's microscope any longer. But if you pictured me with a margarita and my feet up after elimination, you couldn't be further from the truth. After the show ends, they put the losing duo in a car straight to *Jimmy Kimmel Live!* for an interview. Then we're off to LAX for a red-eye to New York, followed by an early-morning interview on *Good Morning America*. My feet were so swollen from six weeks of dancing that I couldn't fit into my heels for those appearances. I had to ice them and find a pair of shoes a size bigger to get through it. It took a little while for my feet to return to normal, one of the souvenirs of being on the show. I wish I could say that another souvenir is that I've held on to that great training and I could teach someone the rumba or the Argentine tango, but I didn't retain much. It wasn't a deliberate learning process as much as it was a mad-dash memorization and boot camp. My parents had a blast with the show. They came every week to watch me perform, and they thought it was a really fun atmosphere.

Now that I was off *DWTS*, Corey wasn't one to admit wrongdoing or to apologize, so I didn't push the issue. The show was over, and we just moved on. I had sprained my ankle during rehearsals, and before each performance, I was wrapping it in numbing bandages. Still though, I was in the best shape of my life and I would do it all over again.

We planned a trip to Hawaii and then on to Australia to visit Corey's family. It was my first trip to Australia, and my first time meeting his family. Even though things were tense before we left, we had such a great time. He was totally different in vacation mode. Anytime I was away from work, we were good. His family seemed really nice, and I really liked who he became when he was around them. He was like a different person—so sweet and so happy, like he just snapped into being a little boy around his mom and dad. I wished he could be like that all the time, but it never seemed to last.

When we started dating, I was in a very busy and exciting time in my life and career. Coming off the end of *The Hills*, followed by *Dancing with the Stars*, I was often being followed by paparazzi or recognized when out in LA. I had agents and publicists calling with opportunities, invitations, and requests regularly. It was incredible! But it also came with a lot of pressure and decision-making, and it could sometimes feel overwhelming to me.

Looking back, I think that Corey thought he could handle being with someone in the limelight. But whereas I could separate my real life from performances, from the "Audrina" you see on TV, he couldn't. It felt like everything he initially loved about me and encouraged me to pursue became what he hated about me. Mentally, it put me in a dark place. I spent a lot of energy trying to figure out what I did wrong and what I could change.

Our relationship was never easy for long. Even during our best times together, I began to feel more like I was holding my breath, waiting for something to set him off. Corey happened to show up at the right time for me to close one chapter of my life and move forward with a new one; to put my time, energy, and focus into our relationship to see if it would actually work out. Because of that I kept justifying his behavior whenever his true colors would shine through. He was slowly showing me who he really was, but I was ignoring it. I wanted to see what I wanted to see. And that willful ignorance would end up costing me.

Chapter Seven

Welcome to the Patridge Family

Soon after my run on *Dancing with the Stars* ended, my new reality show, *Audrina*, began filming. I was exhilarated physically from six weeks of dancing and training, and emotionally exhausted from dealing with Corey's controlling behavior throughout, but, as they say, the show must go on.

After *The Hills* finale and before I could get too comfortable in some time off, an incredible new opportunity came my way. Enter Mark Burnett. For those who don't know, he's a freaking legend and a leading force in reality television. He created and produced *The Apprentice*, and was the executive producer of shows including *Shark Tank*, *Survivor*, and *The Voice*. One of my agents had been quietly floating the idea of a reality show following my family to a few production companies, and it turned out that Mark was very interested.

My agents scheduled a big meeting with Mark and his team so that we could pitch the show in person. I was already nervous, so it was hard to take it as anything but an omen when, on my way to the meeting, I got in a car accident. It was only a fender bender, thank goodness, but with my car broken down on the side of the road, it was quickly looking like my only options were to be terribly late or miss the meeting entirely. Luckily, I called my brother, and he was able to drive to meet me at the crash site. He took care of my damaged car while I got in the other car—and made it to the meeting with Mark on time. I still owe my brother for that.

Thankfully, the accident wasn't an omen of worse things to come. In the meeting, I pitched a show that would follow my family as we lived our daily lives and navigated family dynamics, all while I pursued my career as a host, model, and actress. After *The Hills*, where I was really part of a big ensemble, the show would focus exclusively on me and my family. It might not have been as creatively fulfilling as the acting and hosting I was hoping to get into, but I knew it would be great for my career. After the pitch, Mark was in. The show was green-lit, and *Audrina* would move forward on VH1.

At first my parents were hesitant to be on a reality show. They'd seen my experience on *The Hills*—for better and for worse—and they weren't jumping at the thought of being followed by cameras, constantly mic'ed, and encouraged into dramatic confrontations. They'd watched me struggle occasionally when I felt I was not being portrayed accurately, but then they also saw how incredible it was for my career. So they agreed to do it, mostly for me. They liked the idea that people would get to see the "real" me and my family life. They knew it would be good for me professionally too. Then I had to get my siblings on board. My youngest sister, Samantha, hates reality TV and didn't want any part of it, but she came around by the end of the season and appeared in a few episodes. We filmed her sixteenth birthday on the show, and you can see my mom's over-the-top party planning in action. My sister Casey was down to do it too. She had appeared on *The Hills* several times with me, so she knew what she was getting into. We're so close in age (she's just fifteen months younger) and we'd always been tight growing up, best friends who told each other everything. I was looking forward to spending more time with her while we filmed *Audrina*. Over the last few years, I had been working and away a lot, and I probably hadn't made as much time as I should have to visit her, but we still talked all the time and stayed connected. My brother, Mark, is so low-key, so he just said yes and went with the flow.

I had seen relationships torn apart by *The Hills*, but I truly thought this would be different. It was our family, bonded by so much more than a group of twentysomething friends. I had producing credits on *Audrina* and I thought I would have a creative say on the storyline. I get that, on a reality show, no one wants a happy-go-lucky storyline. They had to get the most drama out of it. I thought with my family the show would feature more normal everyday life, but that's not great TV.

We filmed for three months—so short compared to *The Hills*, which had the cameras rolling almost year-round. I thought it would be fun and relaxing, filming in our family home among the people I'm closest to, but the truth was: it ripped my family apart. My family had no idea what they were walking into. They'd watched enough of *The Hills* to have a sense of what the experience would be like; but when you're not on-camera, in the thick of it, you have no idea how the drama and stakes can be framed. I would always tell them "just be yourself," but it's hard to be yourself when the cameras are on and producers are prodding you to say certain things. Even in the comfort of your own home, the bright lights and prying eyes of producers can be intimidating. One of the day-to-day showrunners was very manipulative and purposefully created drama to juice up ratings, often telling my mom one thing and my sister Casey another to pit them against each other.

They've always had a tense relationship, partially because they're so similar. My sister wanted her own storyline on the show featuring her husband and kids, and it didn't sit well with her when the focus was on our immediate family. Meanwhile, my mom was always so nervous filming that she would have less of a filter and a short fuse, and ended up being harder on Casey. Production managed to get everyone so riled up it was like a powder keg ready to blow.

It was so tough for me to see the fallout from this show within my own household, and it only got worse over the course of filming. It's one thing when it's petty he said/she said drama between twentysomethings with low stakes; it's quite another when it's a mother and daughter with a history of tension in their relationship blowing up in front of the cameras. I've always tried to be the peacemaker between the two of them, but as much as I would try to de-escalate things, I also had to let them feel their feelings and go through it. It was devastating, and I hated to see it happening.

I knew early on that the show couldn't continue beyond the few months we'd already agreed to film. I didn't even want the remaining episodes to air. I would rather have had the show just cut off than my mom and sister have to relive their horrible arguments. Obviously, a second season was out of the question for me. The experience was so traumatizing for the family that I've vowed never to bring people that I truly love and care about onto a show again. It's never worth it.

Casey didn't talk to my mom for a year after we were done filming, and she was furious at me for a long time because she was convinced that I'd had production edit the show to make her look bad. If I'd had any power over the editing at all, the opposite would have been true: none of her blowups with my mom would have made the final cut. The show ripped our family apart for at least a year. I kept reaching out to my sister regularly, and eventually, because time heals, she was willing to talk.

Of course, it wasn't just about Casey and my mom. If you're familiar with *Audrina* at all, then you know one of the things my family fought about was my relationship with Corey. My family had a lot of reservations about Corey and the way he treated me when we were filming.

My family really got to know him during those long days of shooting *Audrina*, and their concerns about him loomed large. We were dealing with a lot as a family under the bright lights and scrutiny of reality TV, yet the concern over Corey's behavior was palpable. Corey was based near Orange County during those months of filming, so when he wasn't traveling, he was around a lot more. For the first time, they saw how he really treated me. They saw the demands that he made of me, the unrealistic expectations on my time and energy, and—maybe most of all—the way it affected me. But they also saw Corey share his feelings for me honestly and genuinely, and be present and open with our family. They saw the bad, but they saw that it wasn't all bad. I think that, by the end, they were just as confused about him as I was.

Casey knew more of the details than anyone in my family. We talked a lot, especially while I was dealing with so much Corey drama, and I confided my darkest secrets in my sister. It was so hard for her to see how loving and kind he could be to me in front of the cameras or other people, and know that behind closed doors it was different. Casey made her feelings about him very clear on-camera, as did several of my closest friends. She was vocal in what she thought about him when things were rough with us, and even during his periods of loving behavior, she remained skeptical.

Whenever Corey came to visit, it seemed like he expected me to drop everything in my life to be with him. It was fun to fill my days with that relationship just after *The Hills* ended and I was looking for something to do, a way to spend my time. But once I got back into a work routine, it just wasn't realistic. I was still trying hard to build a career as a model, actress, and host. And

I was doing it too! But success wasn't just being handed to me. I had to take meetings and be on shoots and auditions, and whenever I was out of the house for longer than an hour or two, all of Corey's *Dancing with the Stars* insecurities came flooding back. I was at a photo shoot for *Marie Claire* magazine—a *huge* get—and he was texting and calling the whole afternoon of the shoot. The messages grew more urgent and angrier; not only did I find it distracting, but the other people on set started to notice how his obsessive, controlling behavior was affecting me too. It was only a few hours, but he was still furious that I wasn't getting back to him right away.

I started to feel smothered by his desire for control, which slowly started seeping into other aspects of my life. He once asked me to delete my Facebook account to prevent me from connecting with people he didn't know or approve of, and to stop anyone from sending me messages. In retrospect, it's clear to me that he was trying to cut me off from my friends, to isolate me so that he was the only person in my life I could turn to. It's also clear that he didn't trust me.

I can't quite explain why this didn't lead me to break up with him. Looking back on it now, it's embarrassing to remember that time and how I acted. It was as if I was able to block out or separate this egregious behavior from the Corey I wanted to be with. I don't know if I have any easy explanations to share in this book. I'm still trying to understand, and working through it in therapy. I was holding on to the way that he was when it was good, when he was on his best behavior and he was loving and fun and affectionate. Now, of course, I can see that I was giving him way too many chances. But that's how I was with Justin too. I wanted it to work out, so I overlooked a lot of bad behavior. I bent my own instincts and inner voice to make the situation work, until I bent enough that I lost the ability to stand up straight for a while.

It also didn't help that, frankly, I started to get used to those ups and downs with Corey, and the lows didn't quite seem as low the next time around. The highs didn't feel as high either, but I thought that was just us mellowing into a new sense of "normal." It became so normal that I started to worry when we *weren't* going through that turbulence. Today, I would call this emotional blackmail, and I think a lot of women who go through it feel like they're groomed by their partner to tolerate increasingly bad behavior. It becomes almost like a spell or a mind trick, when you can no longer figure out what's right and wrong, or how to articulate your own emotions. Everything you do is to keep your partner happy, to stay in the upswing of that roller-coaster ride.

To add insult to injury, I also found out he was cheating on me. We had been dating for almost a year, and everything felt great between us to me at the time. We were both asleep one night when I was woken up by Corey's phone, which kept going off. I just wanted to go back to sleep, so I walked over to his side of the bed to turn his phone off, or at least make sure that there wasn't an emergency. Somehow, I think I knew what was happening, and that I needed to see it for myself; otherwise I would have just woken him to deal with it.

I looked down and saw a bunch of messages coming in all at once, and all from a girl I'd never heard of. I knew Corey's password, but I'd never used it before. I honestly didn't want to know. But now I was curious, and I also knew that if I didn't look I'd spend the next week wandering around with these messages on my mind. So I unlocked his phone and read them.

Immediately, I saw multiple photos of a woman, completely naked, with her legs spread. Maybe this was a mistake, I thought. Maybe she thought she was texting someone else, or she'd been coming on to him but he'd politely turned her down before. I scrolled up. There were plenty of texts from Corey, like: "Baby, come on, send another one, that's so hot." I was white-hot with anger, but not surprised. After pushing aside my suspicion for a while, now I knew.

I woke him up and showed him the phone as he blinked up at me, groggy. I held up the phone and demanded: "Who the fuck is this? How could you do this? How long has this been going on? You're such a fucking liar."

Corey was dumbfounded at first, but as soon as he fully woke up, he returned fire. "You're crazy! What are you doing, snooping through my phone? You're such a jealous bitch."

I yelled for him to get out of my house, but he refused. Of course—he was so stubborn, he would never leave. But that didn't mean I had to stay. I slept in the guest room that night. The next morning, I got up and left early to go to work. I didn't answer his calls or texts for a few days and took some time apart. But he wouldn't leave me alone. He wouldn't stop. He wouldn't give up on me.

Finally, just to get him to stop, I picked up. He immediately started sobbing, telling me that it would never happen again, and that he was so, so sorry. I told him I needed some time alone to think about it and hung up.

When I found out that he was cheating, when I saw the naked photos and the sexting between them, I told my family about it. It put a bad taste in their mouths, to say the least. He was controlling and demanding, often wanting me to cancel work obligations to spend time with him when he was in town. He was so possessive, always asking me who I was spending time with and texting. My family knew me and they couldn't understand why Corey was so untrusting and jealous.

For the show, I was invited as a special guest to the International Polo Club in Palm Beach, Florida, with my brother and one of my girlfriends, Joey. I was supposed to bring Corey, but obviously I wasn't going to do that now. The trip came at the perfect time for me to get away. I was offered the chance to try polo, and that's when I met Nic Roldan, one of the polo players. We immediately hit it off. Sure, it was a little flirtatious, but nothing inappropriate. After all, we were being filmed. More than anything, flirting with Nic reminded me that it was fun to talk to an interesting guy who was also interested in me.

But no amount of harmless flirting went unpunished with Corey. The paparazzi had captured Nic giving our little group a polo lesson, including the two of us riding in the saddle together. By that evening, those pictures had made it online, and Corey was furious. He called me dozens of times that day. *Literally dozens.* I later found out that when he couldn't get hold of me, he called my mom, my dad, and Casey.

I felt sick to my stomach when I saw how many times he'd called. This was bad. Missing those calls and hearing the angry messages from Corey immediately put me back in the mindset of not wanting to make him angrier.

The next morning, I knew, I would have to face the music. He called again, and when I picked up, my hands were trembling. He immediately started screaming at me and ranting: "Who were you with? Where did you go? How late did you stay out?" I was so tired of being interrogated like a criminal. I told him I didn't want to engage in this conversation, and he told me that I lacked compassion, that he'd been up all night worrying because he hadn't heard from me. It was a classic Corey manipulation tactic, to turn everything around on me. He plays the victim so I can't get mad. When I try to stand up for myself, to express my side of the dispute, he'll say things like, "Why are you getting so aggressive right now? I just want to talk."

I always told myself that I would never let a guy control me. But I could see in moments like this that not only was I letting it happen, but I wasn't even putting up much of a fight. I didn't like how I felt, but I was still torn. I loved him enough that I didn't feel my path forward was clear.

Eventually I managed to end the call with Corey without having had much of a chance to explain myself. And when I got home from Florida, he was sitting in front of my house, head in his hands, radiating despair. It was sad and pathetic, but it also hit me with this deep ache: I could help him, heal him, and love him when he needed it. I was able to muster up my strength and walk inside without engaging him that day, but he persisted, parking in front of my house for days, sleeping in his car, refusing to leave unless I would talk to him. So I did, and it was the same conversation that we'd had over and over and over: he was sorry, he wouldn't do it again, but also, if I could just be better for him, he wouldn't need to do these things. Somehow, I held my ground.

After that, Corey had to travel for work, and it gave me the space to feel my feelings without him hanging over me. I had continued talking to Nic a little after we'd filmed, and he actually came out to visit me in Hermosa Beach. It was nothing serious; both of us were dealing with ongoing drama from past relation-ships. But it was a nice flirtation and a really welcome diversion from all of the heavy scenes with Corey. I even brought Nic to a barbecue with my family, so he got to meet everyone, and we took a trip to Cozumel to get away and enjoy some time together. It was fun, but I wasn't reading too much into it, just enjoying the moment. Nic might have felt differently, though. I realized that he was looking for something more when he invited me to Argentina to meet his family. I needed to stop sending him mixed messages, so I backed off.

The end of *Audrina* was also the end of me and Corey. Our breakup was captured on the final episode of the show, and his emotional reaction was genuine. It was one of the strangest scenes I'd ever filmed. We were supposed to meet in a private room in the back of a bar, and he seemed surprised that there were cameras there. He said he didn't want to have this conversation on TV. We had been talking and seeing each other on and off for almost three years, and his reaction made me think that this was finally it for us. I told the cameras in my finale that everything I had felt for him was dead—but that wasn't true.

My heart—and my head—were so turned around and confused by the back-and-forth. I was caught in the riptide, tumbling and tumbling, hoping to find the water's surface.

· Chapter Eight ·

Falling in Love Is Hard to Do

When *Audrina* came to a close, I was single, reeling from the drama within my family and from the dramatic breakup with Corey. I wanted to focus on what was next professionally, and I wanted to get back on solid ground emotionally. It was nice to have some time and space to myself again. I focused on work, and on spending time with friends, enjoying my life.

Then Corey's grandfather died. He was back in SoCal when he got the news, and in early 2012 he reached out to me for support. I was never close to Corey's family, but part of me wishes I'd reached out at some point and told them what was really going on. Did they know how cruel and aggressive he could get? Did they know about his temper? I felt like I was completely alone in dealing with his volatility. Even if I did reach out, I don't know what they could have done except maybe help me feel like I was a little less crazy or a little less alone.

Once, when we were visiting Australia to celebrate his birthday with his family and friends there, we were at a hotel for the party, and when we got into an argument, he left the party to sulk in his room. I was upset, and I felt the need to tell his family what our relationship was really like. It's hard to put on a smile and pretend everything is perfect all the time. So I thought they should have a little context. I told them that Corey was sending naked photos and sexting with other girls, and they made it into a joke, like it was some "boys will be boys" type of thing and that made me feel uncomfortable for making a big deal out of it. That wasn't okay with me.

When Corey reached out in need, I felt a lot of pressure to be there for him, and my compassion outweighed my desire for a clean break. No matter what we'd been through, I felt for him during such a tough time, so I let him come over to talk and I offered my condolences.

Maybe you can see how manipulative and crazy and sick this is, but I would look into the big brown eyes of the only man who'd ever said he loved me openly and emphatically, and my heart would break to see him in pain. To see someone so strong, so together, so accomplished, break down crying and begging felt real to me. And I wanted to be there for him.

After we spoke, Corey was off to Australia to be with his family. When he got back to California, he reached out again and told me, earnestly, that his grandfather's death had changed him. It made him realize that he didn't want to lose me, and how important I was. I wasn't sure that I was ready to be back with him, or even that I wanted to. But it was enough to make me take his calls again.

For the next several months, he was on his best behavior, with the full-court press of Corey charm. Somewhere in my head I knew that he was using his grandfather's death as a way to get back together. But, damn, that charm was so intoxicating. It was such a relief to be dating privately, without the cameras rolling. There was no pressure from producers to go on a date and talk about whether or not we were exclusive, for example. I could really focus on him and let things develop naturally. We started hanging out more and more, just the two of us, and I was always over at his place. When we were together, it was good. Corey made me feel so seen, so cherished. He was generous with his attention and affection. Still, we were reluctant to give ourselves a label. I ignored my nagging feeling, just like I ignored the cheating.

Because of course there was more cheating. It wasn't just the one time captured on *Audrina*. I later found out that when he was traveling month in and month out, he wasn't being loyal. Once our relationship went public on *Audrina*, I started receiving a few messages from girls on Twitter telling me that their best friends were making out with Corey at a party in Oregon or Florida or Oklahoma. The messages were all the same: they wanted to let me know because they were fans of mine and the show and didn't want to see me get hurt. If only they knew.

I did confront Corey, but he'd just say that these were stupid girls who were lying for a chance to interact with me. He called me gullible for believing them and accused me of never having his back. Once again, Corey would turn it around on me, acting hurt that I didn't believe him. But here's the thing: I never dealt with fans reaching out about cheating when I was with Justin or Ryan. Not once.

In my heart and in my gut, I felt that these women were telling the truth. It just seemed too bizarre for them to go out of their way to get in touch and provide such specific information if they were making it up. Plus, the details really seemed to line up.

The pattern went like this: Corey would have to travel for work again, and I would throw myself back into my own work, doing appearances and photo shoots. I could almost robotically shut down the emotions I was experiencing and seem present, engaged, and happy while at work.

But after a period of not talking and being apart, we would slowly start talking again. I couldn't deny that he knew me better than anyone else, and he would often confess his feelings for me during one of our late-night phone calls. Then we would get back together when he was in town, and he would be on his best behavior, making all kinds of promises and resolutions. He vowed to do better and be better. Sometimes he would sit on my doorstep for the better part of several days until I would finally give in, or call so many times that I would answer just to get it to stop. He would keep it up for a while, and somehow I wouldn't be angry. Corey was part of my life, and I learned to adapt rather than shut him out completely as I now know I should have. If this is all starting to sound a bit repetitive, you're not wrong. It's hard to keep straight all of the breakups and reconciliations we went through during those few years.

The pattern continued: he'd be great, and then something would happen. He'd accuse me of talking to other guys at a photo shoot or an event, and when I denied it, he'd yell and scream and punch doors. Or he'd be traveling and I wouldn't hear from him for days at a time, which usually meant he was cheating on me. I'd give him the benefit of the doubt until I got curious when he was home and checked his phone, when I'd invariably see photos of naked girls or sexts. Every time I confronted him, it would be my fault. I didn't love him enough or I didn't answer his calls when I was out to dinner or at an event. His cheating was because of whatever I did to trigger him. It was always my fault.

The sheer number of breakups couldn't have been healthy for either of us.

And so, yes, eventually we slowly started talking again, but I didn't tell anyone. If that's not a sign right there . . . I see now that I forgive and forget too easily.

But, after all of this time, something had changed. I didn't want the ups and downs anymore. And I didn't want to live a life without Corey either. So, what did I do? I made him happy. I put him first, always. I answered every phone call, checked in with him, stayed away from even talking to other men at work events. Even writing this makes me sick to my stomach now, but

I thought it was the only way that we could move forward and truly be happy together.

And the thing is, it worked. Corey and I became more serious, and we were almost inseparable. I stopped working so much in order to spend more time with him, traveling to Australia to see his family and to support him at his competitions. I turned down amazing opportunities for roles in movies and different TV shows, like an HBO comedy called *Blue Mountain State*. He made such a big deal over the male actors starring in the show. To avoid conflict, I decided not to take the meeting. I remember my whole team—my agents, my manager, my lawyer, everyone—was so upset with me because I was sacrificing these important opportunities for him. I didn't care. I was so blindly in love.

Still, I knew I wanted to be focusing on acting and that doors were opening for me as *The Hills* gained more traction. I was getting to audition for great roles in bigger productions, whether it was a guest spot on *Two and A Half Men*, or a role in the blockbuster movie *Burlesque,* alongside Cher and Christina Aguilera. I didn't get those parts, but I was happy to be in the mix and auditioning. I was so nervous for the *Burlesque* audition that I drank coffee beforehand, which I don't normally do, thinking that it would help me focus. Instead, I was even more nervous and shaky from the caffeine, and I definitely didn't bring my A game. I auditioned for the role that ultimately went to Julianne Hough, and as much as I loved the script, losing out on a dancing role to an elite professional dancer seemed fair enough. I did land a small part in *Scary Movie 5* in 2013, and I loved it. The *Scary Movie* scene was a spoof of *Fifty Shades of Grey* that I did with Kendra Wilkinson and Jerry O'Connell, and it was later cut and released as part of the deleted scenes. Corey knew, of course, that I was filming the movie, but I didn't give him details on the scene until after it was already done. I never even saw the final scene, since it was released as part of the DVD outtakes.

This continued with almost everything I auditioned for or took a meeting about. The accusations of flirting or keeping secrets were exhausting. He didn't want me to go to certain auditions because of handsome costars, others if there was a romantic scene. To put it as bluntly as possible: I felt like my relationship was destroying my career. I was putting my relationship and validation from a man above all else. I was in high gear trying to get opportunities and make connections in acting and hosting. But I would *always* turn projects down if I felt they would cause conflict for us. At the time, I thought that it was just him being passionate and mildly controlling. Looking back, I have no doubt that Corey was reducing the scope of my world so that it revolved around him and nothing else.

After years on *The Hills*, I was comfortable in front of a camera. I enjoyed that feeling of improvising with the cast and being ready for anything. So I started hosting a few red carpets, including one for MTV, but I quickly found that it wasn't for me. The questions I was being told to ask seemed invasive, sometimes pulled from tabloid headlines and rumors, or overly personal for a thirty-second sound bite. When I was walking the carpet myself, I hated being asked those personal questions, so I always cringed when I had to ask them. I just didn't enjoy sticking the mic in someone's face. But I'm glad I tried it out.

Then in 2014, my agent called with some great news for me on the hosting front. She told me about an NBC travel show called *1st Look*, and said they were interested in me being their next host. She warned me: it wasn't the cushiest job in terms of pay and perks, but it gave me the opportunity to get into hosting and travel. I jumped at the chance. For the next two years, I was home for four days a month, and traveling the rest.

The show was a dream come true. *1st Look* had been around for a while, since 2008, with different hosts throughout its run. It's on NBC, typically airing late Saturday nights after *Saturday Night Live*. It's an experiential travel series that takes viewers around the world in search of the best places to eat, play, and indulge. I threw myself into work, soaking up these amazing new experiences as I traveled all over the country, from Seattle to the Florida Keys. I hoped this would be the start of something new and challenging, and I could see myself doing it for a long time.

My life on the road filming *1st Look* was really simple, and I loved it that way. I focused on the task at hand, prepared for that day's setup, filmed and interviewed as needed, and enjoyed collaborating with the production team, which was constantly pushing me to trust my instincts. The days were often long, and there were usually multiple locations throughout the day, so it was a lot of changing outfits and moving from place to place. I had to be focused and ready to jump into any situation that might come up. Usually, after a full day of filming, the crew would all go get dinner together and talk about what the next day was going to bring. I was seeing parts of the country and the world I'd always imagined—Chicago, Miami, Seattle, New Orleans—and it was just incredible. We even took an amazing two-week trip to South Korea, where I ate and drank my way through the busy, energetic streets of Seoul, and even tried diving for fresh seafood. The street food scene is big there, and I had a blast trying different kinds of foods with the guidance of the show and our guests.

When I had time off from *1st Look*, I caught up with friends in LA and my family in OC and tried to enjoy myself. I even met a few new guys and went on a few dates.

I had known Chace Crawford for many years after being connected by his manager. Early in my *Hills* stint, I was with Lauren in New York, and we went to dinner with Chace and his *Gossip Girl* costar Blake Lively. It was a lovely dinner with sangria at a trendy Spanish restaurant downtown. *Gossip Girl* had recently premiered and *The Hills* was a year or two into its run, so we were all kind of newbies and hanging out. Later on, Chace and I saw each other at various awards shows or Hollywood events, sometimes out at clubs or at mutual friends' parties. We weren't in touch directly, but we definitely socialized in similar circles and would catch up a little each time.

Then, while I was on break from filming *1st Look*, I ran into him in Malibu at a friend's house, and what can I say—sparks were flying. We ended up staying there with our friend at this gorgeous mansion right on the beach for a long weekend, and we were just inseparable. That's kind of the thing to do in the summer. A lot of people get out of LA and spend time in Malibu, party-hopping and crashing with different friends. While we spent our days playing pool and swimming, Chace and I really connected, and took our friendship to another level. I genuinely liked him after these incredible few days together, and I had the feeling it was mutual.

When it was time to head back to LA, Chace offered to give me a ride, but I went with another friend instead. We made promises to get together soon. And when I got home, Corey was sitting in front of my house, where he stayed for the next three days. I'm so glad I didn't let Chace drive me home; I can only imagine the scene if he had dropped me off with Corey waiting out front.

Yes, I know what you're thinking—and believe me, I get it. A big part of me wishes I'd told Corey to kick rocks and just gone out with Chace. He's such a gentleman and so normal and kind. It would have been fun, if only I hadn't let Corey back in and screwed up our chance.

Corey and I were still in touch, believe it or not. (I'm sure, at this point, you can believe it.) While I was on the road with *1st Look*, there was something so comforting about having someone to call or text and check in with as I worked and traveled alone. And he was also traveling the world competing in BMX for six to seven months of the year, so he understood everything I was going through in a way that nobody else did. Still, I wouldn't say we were back in a relationship. Whenever he was in town, we would jump at the chance to see each other, but then he'd leave, and I'd leave, and we would return to our own separate lives—

mostly. His controlling tendencies would still flare up, and if I didn't pick up the phone or message him back promptly, he'd ask me if I was hooking up with the producers or partying too hard.

Before long, I got sucked back in. I was lonely on the road all the time, and he was always there to talk. I started my bad habits and routines again, like always answering whenever he called and telling him everything I was doing and who I was with at all times. If I told him that the whole crew had gone to a late dinner and then karaoke as a group, he would use it against me to pick a fight. Corey was good at setting rules and boundaries for me, and even better at enforcing them. But he didn't play by his own rules. I knew that he was still partying and talking to girls when I was away.

The distance of traveling and the distraction of working eventually gave me the strength to see this ridiculous double standard for what it was, and I cut it off. In 2015, toward the end of filming my second and final season of *1st Look*, we broke up over the same old stuff—but this time, it wasn't just a pause. I really saw this as a genuine "this is the end" breakup. Which was perfect timing, because shortly after that, I found myself in New York for a while filming a few episodes of *1st Look*. I was enjoying my time in the city, filming and trying new restaurants and clubs. I felt really free for the first time in a while, energized by the city. Then one night—this is crazy—I ran into Justin at this little dive bar downtown. I was just happy and excited to see someone so familiar. Justin had been living in New York for a while, and we decided to meet for drinks and catch up while I was there.

Justin seemed really centered and happy. I couldn't help but tell him: "You're a completely different person now." He told me that I was too. We met up a few times while I was there. It felt good to spend time with him—both familiar and different, as we'd both grown up so much in the years since I last saw him at *The Hills* wrap party. Then I went back to LA, and Justin stayed in New York.

I wasn't surprised to hear that Justin thought I seemed different. When I was traveling and away from my normal routines and social circles in California, I really did some soul searching. I got my confidence back, and for the first time in a while, I felt like I really knew who I was and what I wanted. The producers from *1st Look* brought something out of me that I didn't know I had. They helped me find my natural abilities to express myself and connect with others. They reminded me that people actually cared about what I had to say, and that I didn't need to hold back. I realized that I had begun to question every single thing I wanted to say before I said it, to think and rethink, which led me to say less. It was mostly from filming *The Hills* for so long and not wanting to make a mistake on-camera or say something that could be edited and twisted into something else. But it was also from never wanting to say something that might cause a fight in my relationship.

I sometimes contemplate how Corey became the one who ended up penetrating my walls, the one I stuck with through so many years and terrifying moments of anger. The funny thing is, I think it's because I felt safe with him. He was very protective (what I thought was protective), and at the time, I really needed security. I had (and still have) a restraining order against a stalker who used to come to my house all the time, and who threatened to kill me in a series of letters, poems, and drawings left on my doorstep. The last time he showed up at my house, I arrived home in a car service after a press junket and saw him standing in front of my house with a backpack. I told the driver not to stop, but he saw the car and chased us down the road. I called the police from the car, and when they arrested him on my property, it turned out he had knives in his backpack. For a while after that I was afraid to be alone. With Corey, I knew that he would always be there to protect me if anything bad happened.

I got so used to his company that I always felt like something was missing without him. He was very persistent, and very charming in everything he did. He exercised so much admirable control in his training and his career. But the flip side of that was the control he wanted to exert over me; the way he tried to discipline me when I didn't behave as he desired; and the intensity, vitriol, and manipulation that ultimately broke me down.

Which is why, even though we'd really broken up that last time, I heard his voice in my head more and more with each passing day. I wanted it to work out for us. I wanted to be happy, in love, and secure in my relationship. If only I could want it enough to make it true.

· *Chapter Nine* ·

Entering Mama Bear Mode

After I finished filming *1st Look*, I returned to Orange County. I loved all of the travel experiences—meeting new people, seeing new places—but after spending so much time away from home, I was really looking forward to some time off to relax and catch up with my family. I was single again, and after a few great weeks in New York, I was feeling solid and confident, ready to be back home and starting fresh.

Pretty soon after I got back, guess who was calling me? You got it: Corey. Just when I was feeling good, he was back. He called me to come pick up a bunch of stuff I had left at his house. When I got there, it was clear he was also hoping to talk. We were sitting in his kitchen catching up a little when I got a phone call from Casey that my aunt Darla had died. She was only in her late forties, and in good health—she had a blood clot in her lungs and died quite suddenly. I was shocked and just broke down, sobbing so hard that I couldn't breathe. I hung up and knew I needed to get to my family at the hospital, but I couldn't even form a sentence, much less drive. Corey immediately took over and guided me into his car to get me to the hospital. He knew my family well, and he was supportive and comforting to all of us as we gathered at the hospital to say good-bye.

I was in a very bad place for the next couple of weeks, and Corey was there for me every single step of the way. He literally would not leave my side: he made me breakfast, brought me water, checked on me, and always asked how I was feeling. My whole family was really torn up after her death, and Corey was a shoulder for me to lean on. He knew Aunt Darla, and he mourned her passing as well. My family still harbored resentments against Corey from all of the issues we'd had in the past, but this was a vulnerable time. The experience really brought us together. Seeing him with my mom and sisters crying outside of the hospital changed the way that I saw him fitting into my life.

We got back together without really discussing it. Here we go again, back on the roller coaster. We were just . . . together, all of the time, and it felt natural and good. Corey was always there for me when I really needed him, and now I needed him more than ever.

Although tragedy had reunited us, the next few months were some of the best times we'd ever had. Corey was on his best behavior, taking great care of me and making a real effort to connect with my family too. He wasn't traveling, and I was just filming some last pickup scenes for *1st Look* in LA and thinking about my next move. For the first time in forever, it felt like our feet were on solid ground.

One evening, when we'd been back together for a while, we had plans to go on a boat cruise to hear this country band we love, Old Dominion. The night before, I was just feeling off. I'd poured myself a glass of wine, and it tasted terrible. The smell alone made me cringe. I'd been so exhausted lately and figured that had to be it: my body was just run-down and didn't want the alcohol that night. Except, come to think of it, I had felt off for the last few weeks, at least. I had this inkling that something could be up, and since the next night was the highly anticipated boat cruise with friends, I knew I had to find out now before I had a few drinks on the boat. I went to the drugstore and bought a pregnancy test. I specifically wore a baggy sweatshirt and a hat, hoping no one would recognize me and report it to the tabloids.

I waited until the next day to take the test. I just needed a little more time before knowing for sure, even though some part of me already knew. I was scared of what the result could mean because of our troubled history, but I was also hopeful for that reason. The main reason I was scared had nothing to do with Corey; it was simply that I knew how completely a baby would change my life. All of those plans I was making for my career, and hosting, and trying to get into acting . . . they would all, suddenly, be gone. A baby would change everything, wouldn't it?

In the end, I was right: I was pregnant.

I showed Corey the test, and I will never forget the giant smile on his face. He gave me a big hug that made me feel so content in his arms. He was so excited. It was maybe the happiest I've ever seen him. I wanted to jump in and embrace the sheer excitement, but I couldn't shake the worry that the issues in our relationship—the instability, Corey's temper—would make this an uphill battle. Finally, after a day of disbelief, it all started to sink in. Miraculously, when it did, I felt a deep sense of readiness come from within me. I knew that I would give motherhood my all, and that would be enough.

We left for the boat cruise not long after, and we didn't tell anyone we were with. I ordered a cider and just pretended to sip it all night. I feel terribly for whoever tried to make conversation with me that night. I'm sure I didn't hear a single word. The only thing that was running through my head was: *I'm pregnant! Holy crap, I'm pregnant!*

It turned out I was already eight weeks pregnant, and our baby would be arriving in June. I was shocked I was that far along! I hadn't had any symptoms. My lifestyle in general is pretty healthy—I don't drink a lot, especially when I'm home and relaxing, and I don't smoke or do drugs, so naturally I'd been pretty clean for the two months prior. Thank God for that. Our baby was healthy, and my pregnancy was well underway.

Once I found out I was pregnant, everything began to change for me, and everything became about the baby. I was just instantly ready to embrace the entire process. Throughout my pregnancy, I loved watching my belly grow and feeling the little kicks and hic-cups. When we found out from an ultrasound that it was a girl, I was filled with this bright rush of pure joy. I'm such a girl's girl. I love makeup and dressing up and all of those things, and now I would have a daughter to share that with.

For their part, my parents were over the moon about becom-ing grandparents. My mom grabbed me in her arms and said that she knew I would be a great mother. I was so comforted to have her by my side and to have so much support from my family. Still, they had seen some of the ups and downs of our relationship, and they had their reservations about us parenting together. But at that point, Corey was the best he'd ever been, and they'd also seen how he reacted after Aunt Darla's death. They hoped, as I did, that it was the sign of a reformed man.

My dad did have a heart-to-heart with Corey, which I learned about later, to express how important it was that the issues of the past stay in the past, and that taking care of his family should now be Corey's top priority. Corey was very respectful, and from what I heard, it was a productive conversation.

Once the dust settled on our big pregnancy news, the next thought that came to mind was: *If we're really going to do this, then we have to get married.* I couldn't imagine welcoming this baby as a couple but not a family—that's just how I was raised. Even if the wedding would take place after the birth, it was important to me that our child be raised in a home with parents who were married partners. I would do whatever it took to make our relationship work for the sake of the baby.

When I told Corey how I was feeling about getting married, he told me that he couldn't agree more. In fact, almost a year before, he'd bought a ring in Australia with his sister's help, and he'd hung on to it even after we broke up. Even in those dark moments, even when we were separated, he told me he still thought we'd end up together.

In November 2015, just a couple of weeks after we found out we were expecting our beautiful daughter, Corey proposed. We went to one of our favorite restaurants in Orange County, Summit House, where my family and I have been celebrating every big milestone for as long as I can remember. I knew something was up because Corey seemed nervous all night. And, of course, we'd just had the conversation about getting married, so even though I didn't know when exactly he was going to propose, I was certainly on high alert.

When it came time for dessert, the waiter suggested we share the cheesecake and placed a silver platter with a lid on the table. I glanced at Corey, who dropped to his knee, and as I lifted the lid, I saw there was no cheesecake; instead, I was greeted with a little red box atop a bed of roses. He whispered, "We've been together for a long time now, and I love you more than anything. I want to spend the rest of my life with you. Will you marry me?"

Of course, I said yes. And as soon as I did, my entire family popped out from another room in the restaurant to celebrate with us. Corey had invited them as a surprise, and they were waiting to pop the champagne. My parents were genuinely happy, and we all had decided to put the past behind us and believe that everything was going in the right direction. Everything about the proposal was, honestly, perfect, which was no surprise—Corey always knew me so well. The ring was perfect too: a simple, solitary diamond. I had no idea what I wanted, and it's not like we were discussing rings that far in advance, so Corey had been on his own with the design, and he exceeded expectations. I loved the simplicity and delicate style.

All of a sudden, I was twenty-nine years old and about to become a mother and a wife. It was time to reevaluate my priorities and figure out how to create a safe and nurturing environment for our baby. I still wasn't 100 percent sure that I could trust my relationship with Corey—yes, I realize what a red flag that is in retrospect—so I wanted to take control in the areas I could.

Corey was going to be traveling a lot for work over the next couple months, and I knew that I would rather be in Orange County, near my family, than alone in my house in Los Angeles. So I quickly put my house on the market and started looking at new homes in the OC.

The move kept me busy. I may have allowed the stress to become a little too much. Shortly before the holidays, I loaded my car up with presents for my family and brought them to my grandmother's house for our big Christmas celebration. I was carrying the gifts up the walkway and into her house, when I just started gushing blood. I instantly thought that I had lost the baby and was terrified. In a panic, I drove myself home, and Corey immediately drove me to the emergency room, and—thank you, God—our baby was fine. I had just overexerted, an issue that would resolve on its own as long as I quit carrying around boxes of clothes and books. The doctor mandated two weeks of bed rest.

Everyone thinks that sitting in bed or on the couch all day bingeing bad TV, reading, and relaxing sounds pretty great. Until you're forced to do it. I think the recent pandemic has really taught people that a staycation sounds great . . . until you don't have the choice to leave your house. I've always liked to keep busy, and being forced to sit still with all of the emotions and worries running through my mind about the engagement and pregnancy was immensely difficult. I've also prided myself on how independent I am, and this bedrest meant that I had to ask for help and couldn't do everything on my own. It was a tough two weeks, but the baby's health was more important than my churning mind.

In December, I announced my pregnancy to the world on social media. I was a little nervous, but I was going to start showing and I didn't want to feel like I needed to hide or stress about the secret. After the holidays and my bed rest ended, I went to Australia with Corey for three weeks to spend some time with his family. I had been to Australia several times with him over the last few years, but this time, being engaged and pregnant, was different. His family threw a little engagement dinner party for me and Corey, and it was a lovely celebration.

But when we came back from Australia in January, Corey was gone for most of my pregnancy, traveling for another six months to New Zealand, to Prague, to London, to South America—anywhere but Orange County. I was on my own to find a new house and prepare for our baby. I tried not to worry or stress because of what had happened before, but I couldn't help but feel a little lonely. Corey and I were so solid that fall when I got pregnant, but when he went back out on the road, he disappeared. That's when everything started crumbling again.

When he was traveling for competitions and sponsored content creation, Corey often wouldn't call me for days at a time. I thought he'd check in with me—his pregnant fiancée—daily, or respond to my texts at the very least. But no. Then I'd find out he was at the casino all night with his single friends and random girls, gambling until sunrise and then sleeping through the next day. He wasn't even subtle about it; I found out just by checking his friends' Instagrams or Snapchats, where everything was posted for everyone to see. It looked like he was having the time of his life with booze, all-night parties, and tons of different girls hanging on him.

Being pregnant changed my perspective on everything. I felt like my senses were on high alert, and when you're the only one sober in a group of people partying, it really lets you see more clearly. Whenever Corey was in town very briefly during those months, we'd go out with friends, and I would obviously be the designated driver. I often wanted to go home early if I was tired or my feet hurt, but I didn't want to be a buzzkill, and Corey wasn't tuned in to what I needed. Seeing him get drunk, reckless, and mean while I was completely sober was eye-opening. Normally I'd have been drinking with him, and if he said rude things, I would fight back. But now that I was pregnant and sober, I would just stay silent because I didn't want to get into a fight with a drunk man. Which, it turns out, would make him even angrier. He didn't take it out on me as much, but he could be mean and aggressive toward his friends, yelling and calling them names. It really hit home for me to see it while I was sober. Corey wouldn't remember any of it the next day, which enabled him to move on like it wasn't a big deal.

I was so sensitive to his moods. When it was good, we would talk about the baby and our little family, how excited we were, how precious our little girl would be. But I could never truly enjoy those times, because I'd started to realize that the other shoe would always drop.

I prepared myself, mentally, to have and to raise this baby alone. I was still going to marry him—raising our little girl within a traditional family was that important to me—but I started to see that he wouldn't be there when I needed him.

Financially, I had enough in savings and with the sale of my LA home to feel secure that I could take care of my daughter and support us. To reduce my stress levels, I was taking a break from television work that would take me into LA, so while living with my parents and house hunting, I threw all of my energy into nesting. I spent a lot of time in those last weeks and months of pregnancy preparing myself to become a mother, someone responsible for the safety and well-being of a child. I had to be able to say confidently: *I will take care of the baby girl, no matter what, even if it means doing it alone.*

Looking back, it's clear that I wouldn't have been getting all of my ducks in a row to care for my daughter solo if I thought things were fine. I was worried about Corey, about our relationship, about being a mom, about finding a new home for us in Orange County. And then, of course, I was worried about that stress affecting the baby, which only drove my stress levels higher. That was my first lesson in motherhood: there's so much to worry about, even worry itself. I wanted with every fiber of my being for this to work, for us to be a family, but subconsciously, I was preparing for the worst.

I really threw myself into finding a new home in Orange County to bring my daughter home to; I researched different areas, driving around to scope things out. The house hunt became my focal point, because it allowed me to think about something other than my relationship. I ended up finding this beautiful house in Irvine, in a picture-perfect neighborhood with a lot of young families and parks nearby. I just felt in my bones that this was where we needed to be. It was brand-new construction, with a lot of great natural light. The inside was bright and beachy, with light wood floors. And the big backyard was perfect for running around with Kirra one day. This was the house for us.

When I told Corey about the house, he wasn't engaged or decisive, and he made no move to participate in the purchase. So I bought it myself, with my grandpa as my mortgage cosigner. I remember feeling so proud that I'd done it, and that my grandpa was the one by my side. The house was still being built, and our occupancy date was early June, giving us just a few weeks to settle in before the baby arrived.

While I had stepped back from hosting and appearances, I continued working on Prey Swim, a swimwear line that I'd started a year prior. The tabloids called me the Bikini Queen because I was always photographed in bikinis. I love swimwear, but I'm particular about it, and I often struggled to find what I wanted while shopping for new suits. So, I started sketching swimsuits and imagining new fabrics and patterns. I found partners to handle the production and manufacturing side, which are very important, very specific skills, and together we created Prey Swim. I love the creativity and problem-solving required to design swimsuits, and I look forward to my time in the office, going through designs, working with the fit models, and overseeing fulfillment and shipping. This was also work I could do close to home in Orange County and largely on my own schedule, unlike the demands of Hollywood, so it would be a perfect fit for me when the baby arrived.

I also threw myself into planning a wedding. We decided to get married in Hawaii, which is halfway between our two families. I went to Hawaii several times to plan the wedding, including a few trips with my sister Samantha, who lived on Oʻahu full-time. In the months leading up to the event, I'd look forward to the quick trips to Hawaii to scout venues and bands. Samantha would meet me in Kauai, and we would get everything done on our list and then steal some time at the beach to relax and catch up.

Once I had the venues narrowed down, I took Corey along with me the last time, to show him the final two location options in Kauai. It was going to be a weeklong stay for everyone, an opportunity for our two families to spend some time together before the wedding, so it wasn't a simple affair. I chose the location for the ceremony, the flowers, and the décor; I booked the block of hotel rooms and beachside house rentals, and arranged every single thing, down to cobalt-blue napkins. It was fun, and I'm certainly lucky that I got to have a seaside wedding in paradise. I really enjoyed the planning process.

It's clear to me now that I was looking for distractions and wanted to stay busy. I launched a swim line, moved into a new house, and planned a destination wedding all while pregnant. I didn't want to sit still with my feelings.

When the house was finally ready, I was eager to get in and get settled. I was thirty-seven weeks pregnant and ready to nest before it was time for the baby to arrive. The weekend of our move, when the moving company was bringing all of my belongings in from storage and we were still in major unpacking mode, Corey announced that he was going to Vegas with a few of his friends. The baby was due in a week or two, which meant, realistically, that she could come anytime. I really wanted everything to be unpacked before the baby arrived so that we could focus on her instead of completing the move. As gently as possible, I told him no: "I need you here. I can't unpack all of these boxes by myself. Can you please just stay with me to make sure you're here when the baby comes?" Of course, he didn't think it was a big deal. He said we'd get to it next week, and off he went.

Surprise, surprise—I didn't hear from him for two or three days after that. I soon found out that he was up all night partying hard and going to strip clubs. Then he missed his flight home.

Meanwhile, my family filled the gap and went into overdrive helping me unpack and set up the house. My parents, my siblings, even my grandparents came over to help me go through boxes, get organized, and decorate. We enjoyed making a day of it, taking breaks to prepare and eat a nice lunch. With them, it was starting to feel like home.

My mom was in the front yard when she saw a truck pull up with Corey in the passenger seat. As soon as he saw her, they kept driving, right past the house. When my mom came inside and told me, I was so livid I could hardly breathe. Who was he with that he had to hide them from my mom? I never found out. When he finally got home, I told him I couldn't deal with this level of stress. It wasn't good for the baby, or for me. Instead of comforting me or assuring me that he would be there from then on, he left and stayed at his friend's house that night.

Kirra's due date was June 27, 2016, but at my doctor's appointments leading up to it, there was increasing concern that she was getting so big that she wasn't turning head-down. I'm a fairly narrow person, and my doctors were concerned that she would stay in this breech position, and that, as a result, her health—or mine—could suffer. To avoid any unnecessary complications, we scheduled a C-section for June 21. I was nervous, of course, but if my doctors believed that was the safest way to bring her into the world, I was all for it.

Then we found out last-minute that Corey had to be in San Francisco doing a BMX photo shoot for a couple of days, so we had to reschedule my C-section for June 24, which meant three more days of discomfort and nerves for me.

On the morning of Friday, June 24, 2016, my baby girl was born. She was perfectly healthy, eight pounds, four ounces. The C-section went smoothly, everything according to plan. And there she was in my arms. Holding her sweet little body for the first time and kissing her silky cheeks just broke my heart and then rebuilt it even stronger. I knew that my life was changed forever, in ways that I hadn't even been able to predict while I was pregnant. Anticipating a baby is one thing. Having her in your arms and smelling the top of her perfect head is another. I felt a "mama bear" mentality take over as I looked into my little girl's sweet eyes. I just couldn't believe how deeply I fell in love with this tiny baby.

My beautiful Kirra Max was partially named for my grandpa Max, who passed away just a month before she was born. We were very close, and I'm so glad I can pass part of his legacy down through Kirra. And her first name has always been one of my very favorites, ever since I was young. There are many different potential spellings of that name, but while I was pregnant, I learned that the most beautiful beach in Australia is named Kirra, so I thought that was a meaningful way to honor her dad and his Australian roots.

Corey also fell totally in love with Kirra. In the hospital, as I recovered from the C-section and learned to breastfeed, we all bonded as a family. Corey was supportive, engaged, and excited.

He was a proud father, and invited all of his friends to visit. He even FaceTimed his family in Australia to show off Kirra.

Those first few days were such a tender time, with Kirra always with me to sleep or breastfeed. I could stare at her for hours, memorizing her tiny fingers and toes, looking into her eyes. She was a ray of pure light and joy, everything else paling in comparison. I didn't know what love was until I held Kirra in my arms. I know that every new parent says that, but I didn't realize how true it was until I was the one experiencing it. My heart cracked wide open.

When we first got home, my grandma Betty stayed with me at my house to help, and it was incredible having her there. Since my grandpa had just died, it felt like I needed her and she needed me. She helped me give Kirra her first bath. She took care of me too, making me food and teaching me how to care for Kirra. Then, the second week, I went to her house because Corey was on the road for work again. Having an extra pair of hands to help was truly a lifesaver. Otherwise, I would have been completely alone, one week postpartum.

I was upset about Corey leaving for a work trip only a week after Kirra was born, but I understood the importance of his career. For the first time, his absence didn't bother me that much. It could only penetrate so deep. The moment Kirra was born, something in me started to change. I was just so in love with this baby that I didn't care if the whole world burned down around me. It was the first time I've ever experienced that pure and innocent unconditional love. I just cared about this little baby and being the best mother I could be. Everything else mattered a whole lot less.

It only took a few months with Kirra before Corey caught on to this shift. He'd often talk about how I didn't give him enough attention or make time for him. As a result, even when he was home, he was often out hanging and drinking with his friends.

That was fine by me. I was already very used to doing it all on my own, just me and Kirra.

· Chapter Ten ·

Harder Lessons

I'm constantly learning harder and harder lessons in my life, and the last year of my relationship with Corey was the year that taught me the hardest and most valuable lessons of all. Ironically, it was also the year we got married.

From the beginning, I knew that I wanted the wedding to look like a boho-beachy fairy tale. The event space was this beautiful valley by the ocean, lush green and tropical, and you walked down this gorgeous path to get to our ceremony site on the cliffs overlooking the water. I wanted romantic red roses, draped fabrics, and lots of greenery. I envisioned strings of twinkling fairy lights strung up all over our reception tent, to give it an ethereal and magical look. Once those big decisions were made, I let the local wedding planner and venue run with the execution. There was only so much I could do from two thousand miles away, either pregnant or with a newborn.

Sure, maybe I was fantasizing that the wedding would heal some of the rifts in my relationship, but you can put away your tiny violins. I'm still proud that I planned a beautiful wedding in one of the most stunning places on earth—even if it was to the wrong man.

To find my wedding dress, I flew to New York with my sister Samantha during New York Bridal Fashion Week, which is an annual event for wedding dress designers along the lines of fashion week, and I met the designers behind the Australian brand Pallas Couture. They're known for their flowing, romantic designs, and I thought that it would be nice to go with an Australian label as a nod to the groom. I tried on a few different dresses, and although they were all stunning in their own ways, I couldn't quite find the vibe I was looking for, something to look right at home on the beach. We kept trying, but nothing was quite right. Finally they offered to work with me to design my own dress, which sounded like the perfect plan. We talked about what styles and details I liked and didn't like, they took my measurements, and off they went. In the end, they created a dress that was lace and embroidered, with a sheer panel over my legs, a slightly sexy low-cut back, and a delicate train.

We had a block of rooms at a gorgeous resort not far from the wedding venue, and that's where our families stayed for the week, along with most of our friends. Since this was the first time that our two families would meet, we wanted to make the wedding a weeklong "event," with the ceremony itself taking place midweek to ensure that five-month-old Kirra had time to adjust to any jet lag beforehand. Corey's friends, meanwhile, rented a beach house a little farther away, and Corey spent most of his time there. We planned little events for the family throughout the week, including a fun night of drinks and live music in the lobby, and of course, our rehearsal dinner the night before the wedding.

We invited about 150 people total. Since we both come from big families, this meant a fairly small, intimate guest list. I was glad to keep it that way, to be able to really have fun with my family, dance the night away with my little cousins, and, of course, focus on Kirra. Any bigger and I would have felt pulled in a million different directions, trying to visit with all of the groups and making sure that everyone was having a good time.

My biggest concern was keeping the wedding super private, away from the long lenses of paparazzi cameras. On my special day, I didn't want to have to worry about whether paparazzi were poking around, trying for pictures to sell to the tabloids. I specifically chose the venue because it's so private, and the ceremony itself was down a path along the cliffs. Plus, no one knew the exact location! The wedding invitations didn't give any details, and we bused our guests straight from the hotel to the venue. I'd even asked the venue staff and wedding planner to sign NDAs. I thought I had succeeded in keeping our wedding private—until I saw the pictures in the tabloids before my own photographer had even showed me the official wedding photos. I couldn't believe it. It was frustrating and a little violating, but I'm just glad I didn't know it was happening at the time. I later found out that one of Corey's friends sold the address to one paparazzo, who then climbed up the side of the mountain to snap the photos.

Despite my best efforts, it didn't seem like the extra few days in Hawaii before the wedding had gotten the families to bond, unfortunately. At the rehearsal dinner, my family sat on one side and his on the other, and while people mingled, there appeared to be little real conversation going on. Everyone was on their best behavior, which translated to everyone coming across as guarded. There also seemed to be some conflict over Kirra, who obviously had grown up close to my family and was, as a result, very happy and comfortable with my parents and siblings. She was a little more hesitant with Corey's family—who could blame her? They were all strangers to her! I could tell that she was getting overwhelmed as they all passed her around and smothered her in kisses. It was sweet to see how much they all immediately loved her, but I didn't want to risk a breakdown, so at one point I grabbed her and whisked her away to our room for a quick reset.

After the rehearsal dinner, my mom took Kirra back to the hotel, and I joined Corey and our friends at their house. After a drink or two, I left to get Kirra and head back to my hotel room. Corey stayed the night with his friends and kept the party going. After I got Kirra settled in for bed, I could finally sit down and contemplate that I was getting married the next day. Casey stayed with me that night, and she asked how I was feeling. If I was honest with myself, I was uneasy. After the last few days in Hawaii, I wasn't in the best mood. Corey and his friends seemed to be treating our wedding like an excuse to party hard rather than the ceremony of love and unity that I wanted it to be. I tried to be understanding, but there was still something that bothered me.

The truth is, in the weeks leading up to the wedding, we'd reached a major breaking point, and I had nearly canceled the wedding. He'd acted very strangely when I was looking at houses in Orange County while pregnant, and very standoffish when I found the one in Irvine. It seemed as if he had no interest in buying this house together, which was what led me to cosign the mortgage with my grandfather. I wanted the perfect forever home for our family, in a nice, family-friendly community. There was something about our differing priorities at the time, and our history together, that made me feel the need to ask for a prenup. I clearly had reservations. I asked my parents' advice, and with everything that they'd seen between us over the years, it was no wonder they agreed immediately.

So, two weeks before the wedding, Corey and I went to meet with the attorney, who explained the prenup and how it would serve to protect both of us. Corey had agreed to go with me and hear him out. After the conversation, my attorney drew up the documents—and, shockingly, Corey didn't want to sign. He was furious, saying that any prenup agreement meant that I didn't trust him, and if there was no trust between us, then why were we even getting married in the first place?

I said, as calmly as I could, "I'm not marrying you if you don't sign it." And I meant it.

His response was: "I don't give a fuck, then. Cancel the wedding. It's not my money."

It was so hurtful! I broke down crying in our bedroom after the meeting. But because Kirra's future was at stake, not just mine, I stood firm.

I told him how disrespectful it would be to cancel the wedding on short notice because of the prenup, after how much money, planning, and care my family had put into it. And beyond that, I had put so much effort into making our relationship work. I'd changed the type of work I took on to avoid friction and jealousies. I was patient and forgiving when Corey's behavior was hurtful. I was doing everything I could for our family, and that effort spoke for itself.

Eventually, Corey apologized. And then he signed the prenup.

All of that was on my mind the night before the wedding, and when Casey asked me how I was feeling about getting married the next day, I just felt depleted, which didn't comfort her. She saw that I wasn't the happy, blushing bride eager to marry the man of her dreams. She saw how exhausted and sad and beaten down I was at that point. I remember her looking at me with these somber, determined eyes, and saying: "Audrina, you don't have to do this. Let's pack our bags. Mom and Dad can handle the rest of the guests. Let's just get on a plane and go."

I saw her concern, and I have to admit that the offer was tempting. But I just couldn't do that to my family, and to our guests. I knew how much my parents had paid for the wedding, and how much we had all put into planning it. More than that, I felt that my family wanted this to work; like me, they wanted me to build a family with Kirra. I felt I couldn't just walk away without first seeing if we could make it as husband and wife. After my divorce, I came to find out that so many of my friends and family wished they had stopped me and told me they felt like the wedding was a mistake. But they wanted to support me, and they saw how I determined I was to make this relationship work, so they went along with it.

The morning of the wedding, I woke up feeling fine. I was on autopilot. I felt relaxed and focused, just putting one foot in front of the other, which, by that point, I was very good at. I knew that it would destroy me to wake up on my wedding day and feel doubt and fear, so I made the conscious decision not to have those emotions. I pushed them aside and did what I felt I had to do. Just as I did on TV, I was playing the character of "Audrina," and the scene called for a happy bride, smiling and laughing.

I had asked my two sisters, my sister-in-law, and my longtime best friend Kendra to serve as bridesmaids, and we had fun the morning of the wedding getting our hair and makeup done in our matching robes. I was very calm and focused on Kirra, making sure she was happy and got a good nap in before the ceremony began. I wasn't worried about the wedding details, or Corey, or any drama with our families. As for Corey, he was so happy to spend time with all of his friends and family on the island that I don't think he realized I was off.

And then it was time. My hair was curled in flowing waves fit for the beach, and my makeup was done. Kirra and I were both wearing our white dresses.

As I walked down the aisle arm in arm with my dad, I was literally stopped in my tracks, tugged backward by some invisible force. I couldn't take another step. For a second, I thought it was God stepping in and telling me not to continue. My heart started to beat faster as I thought: *Should I run?* It turned out my veil was caught on a rock along the path, and my dad reached down and unsnagged it. As we continued down the aisle, I kept wondering if that was a sign. And, in the end, maybe it was. Those kinds of moments are little winks from God. You just have to learn how to listen to them and to trust your gut. As painful as calling off the wedding would have been, I regret that I didn't do that at the time.

Instead, I stood under the floral arch, on a beautiful cliff overlooking the Pacific Ocean, and held Corey's hands as we looked into one another's eyes and said, "I do." My mom was holding Kirra in the front row, and hearing her sweet babbling was just about the only thing keeping me steady. This was for her. In the middle of the ceremony, Kirra started fussing and reaching for me, so I went to get her from my mom and held her tight, feeling her warm, wiggly body against mine, the weight in my arms keeping my feet on the ground instead of floating up, up, and away.

After our vows, Corey held Kirra, and I looked at the two of them. I hoped and prayed with all my heart that we would be okay. In that moment, I believed we could make it.

The wedding reception went by in a blur. It was held in a gorgeous tent overflowing with flowers and greenery. I had to admit, it was the most romantic, magical setting I could have imagined.

And we had fun! We started the evening with toasts, raising a glass to those who couldn't be with us, including my grandpa Max and my aunt Darla, and Corey's grandfathers. The best man and my sisters gave toasts, then we all beelined to the dance floor.

Kirra enjoyed a little of the party, and then a wonderful family friend took her up to my room to put her to bed. It was nerve-racking to let someone else put her to sleep for the first time, but I wanted her safe and tucked away, so I was grateful for the help.

We had a great DJ, and I danced with my family and friends the whole time, working my way through a few glasses of Pinot Grigio. My mom, my sisters, and a few of my best friends spent the night dancing, and I remember when our throwback jam Ace of Base's "I Saw the Sign" came on, we really got into it. If only I had actually seen the signs.

After the reception ended, our friends and family continued the party down at the beach in front of our hotel, hanging out under this big olive tree. It was a beautiful night, and you could hear the crashing of the ocean as the waves flowed in and out under the twinkle of the stars. Corey and I stayed until the wee hours of the morning, then went back up to my room to pass out. It wasn't exactly a wedding night filled with passion.

Later, my sister Sam told me that it was like I left my body entirely that day. To everyone else it looked like I was functioning normally, but she saw that behind my smile, I was a robot. I had no sparkle or soul in my eyes. That sounds like a pretty accurate description. It's heartbreaking now to think back on that day, how I was following through with something so monumental that I already regretted. It was a big lesson for me about people-pleasing, and if I had listened to my heart instead of doing what I thought other people wanted me to, I know now that I wouldn't have gone through with it. Unfortunately, that realization is too little, too late.

Despite all of the bad that has unfolded between me and Corey since that day, the wedding party itself is an incredible and cherished memory for me and for my whole family. We had an amazing trip, and I spent so much time with my close circle in a beautiful paradise setting. Even Corey and I enjoyed a few special moments together that week, and I know we both found so much joy in being with our families.

The morning after the wedding, we enjoyed the day by the pool with family before heading home to California, where Corey's parents, his sister, and her family visited with us for a couple of weeks. They hadn't yet seen where Corey was living in Orange County, and it was nice to spend some time with his family.

One morning I had to go into the office to work on Prey Swim and deal with a few things that had been put on hold due to the wedding. I asked Corey to watch Kirra. He immediately said that he couldn't because he wanted to go surfing with his friends. Which he did every single day. I tried to smile and adapt, since his parents were there. I told him that I just needed an hour to focus on my work, and that I would come right back for Kirra as soon as I was done. But he doubled down and refused, saying that his plans were just as important. His mom watched the argument unfold, and eventually stepped in and offered to watch Kirra so that I could work and Corey could surf. I was frustrated with him, as always, but hoped that his mom had seen a glimpse of what I usually dealt with and would maybe talk to him about being more present for his family. It was a stretch, but I was hopeful nonetheless.

The irony is that I always thought Prey Swim would give me the most flexibility while pursuing my passion and creativity. Running my own business outside of the long hours and unpredictable schedules of Hollywood would allow me to be a present, hands-on mom in the ways that I wanted, and, honestly, to avoid feeling torn between my work obligations and Corey's needs. I didn't want to have another *DWTS* experience or bail on another audition when he wasn't comfortable. It helped our relationship for a while, until he got so used to everything being about him all the time. Then, anytime that it wasn't, he blew up.

After his family left, we were all out of distractions. There was no more wedding to plan or family in town to entertain. It was just us. He was either completely absent—traveling or hanging with his friends and partying—or too present, hovering over me with a need to control everything, just like the old days. He would interrogate me if I didn't answer my phone quickly enough. It made seeing friends a miserable experience, so I started staying home more. It seemed easier to make Corey happy than to meet my friends for a girl's night and make him angry.

Slowly, it became harder and harder to be with my friends. I didn't want anyone to know about the way Corey treated me, so even when I did manage to break away from him and see them, I was always on guard, pretending everything was fine. I couldn't go out with girlfriends, have a few glasses of wine, and pour my heart out. There was just too much emotion lurking below the surface for me to open up, and if anything came out, I knew I would break. The hardest thing was, even if I did say something, I didn't know if people would believe me. Everyone else saw him as this charming, good-looking, happy guy. I was afraid that if they heard how much I was struggling, they'd think that *I* was the problem, not him. Eventually, even I started wondering if I was the problem, making things more difficult than they needed to be. My doubt was at an all-time high, and I felt I had nowhere to turn.

All I wanted was for my little family to be together, safe and happy, in a loving home. But as each day passed, that was becoming less and less of a possibility. I loved Corey and I wanted to be with him, but his erratic behavior, not to mention the constant emotional abuse, came into focus as I started to see things through Kirra's eyes. Becoming a mother helped me gain clarity about the people I want around me, and even more important, the people I want around my child. I never imagined I could love so hard and so much until I had Kirra, and that gave me a new perspective on other relationships in my life.

I started to think about what she would internalize if she grew up seeing and hearing her father treat her mother this way, and how that would affect the way she saw herself as a young woman when she started to date and enter into relationships herself. I can say, without hesitation, that Kirra was my guiding light. As a grown woman, I could deal with everything that he did to me. But I couldn't deal with it shaping my little girl.

The pressures and responsibilities of parenthood can really shine a light on a failing relationship, and as much as I wanted to see my little girl safe in her father's arms, I found myself trusting Corey less and less with Kirra. She was so fragile still, and I often brought her with me wherever I went, even to the occasional dinner with my girlfriends.

One of the experiences that shaped how little I trusted Corey with her came shortly before our wedding when Kirra was a few months old. My two sisters planned a surprise bachelorette celebration in Las Vegas for me, and they had worked it out with Corey in advance to take me away for one night. Honestly, I was overwhelmed at the idea of leaving Kirra for the first time. Okay, I was freaking out a little bit. I settled down and tried to enjoy myself for just this one night, and I realized it was probably good for me. What could possibly happen in twenty-four hours?

But while I was gone, I saw videos on several of Corey's friends' Instagram and Snapchat accounts. They were at our house drinking in the kitchen and getting way too rowdy for my liking. The music was loud. His friend was running around the kitchen naked. I called Corey and could barely hear him over the noise. "Where's Kirra?" I asked. "Why do you have friends over getting wasted in the kitchen?"

He told me that she was sleeping upstairs. But I worried that he didn't have the monitor, or that he would be too out of it if she needed something, and no one would be able to take care of her safely. He told me I was overreacting, to trust him and enjoy my time in Vegas. I was livid. I hardly slept a wink that night and couldn't make it home to her fast enough.

When I got home and finally held my sweet girl in my arms again, I noticed vomit stains in her little bassinet. Clearly she'd thrown up in the night and just laid in it. I yelled at Corey for not watching her, telling him I was afraid she could have choked. He didn't seem very concerned. That was one of the last times I ever left him alone with her. But still, I pushed it aside and continued to focus on our wedding.

It's funny, the way that tumultuous year prepared me for life as a single mom. It was the training I didn't know I would need. I never relied on Corey for anything when it came to Kirra. I made all of her pediatrician appointments, kept track of milestones and medications, made playdates, and kissed away every boo-boo. I learned to never depend on him for anything, because whenever I did, he always let us down. Anytime he was in a bad mood, or I knew he was coming home from a trip, I could start to sense his negative energy approaching. I would pack Kirra up and head to my parents' house for a few days to let the dust settle at home. I was going to my parents' house more and more, and although I'm sure they could sense that something was up beyond typical new mom struggles, I still didn't tell them what was going on. I wanted to reach out and grab my mom's hand and tell her I wasn't happy, but I just couldn't.

Corey was traveling a lot for work, and he was inviting his friends along for the trips. It might sound silly to say this in the context of everything else going on, but, come on . . . I would have liked to go too! We could have made a romantic trip out of it. Believe me, we needed it.

Besides, it's not like our lifestyle gave us ample opportunity for intimacy. We were in two different worlds. Some nights he was out until three or four in the morning and would come home drunk and furious, yelling and accusing me of cheating before heading downstairs to sleep on the couch. I would spend my nights giving Kirra a bath, putting her in bed, and, most of the time, falling asleep with her.

There were good days when he was home and present, and we took long walks together with Kirra in the stroller. We'd sit at the beach and watch her marvel at the sand, or we'd push her on the swings at the playground. The nights when he'd cook dinner while I fed Kirra her little purees were so sweet and so good, and it made me stay for every one of the bad days. He made me feel loved and he made me laugh, except when he didn't.

At the same time, my career was starting to pick up a little as Prey Swim got more attention and I had opportunities that came with being a new mom, including pregnancy and motherhood interviews. I always included Corey in the opportunities that came my way, like the pilot for a reality show focusing on celebrity families, which we filmed but unfortunately wasn't picked up. Corey was all for it when it was about him, but when it wasn't, he went on the offensive.

That spring of 2017, as a newlywed with an almost one-year-old at home, I started to go to therapy by myself. I really wanted to give it my all with Corey before even thinking about walking away, but I was starting to realize I had to get out. During a few productive talks, I told Corey that I wasn't happy or getting what I needed. Corey told me he wasn't happy either. He said he wasn't getting enough attention or what he needed from me in our marriage. He agreed to go to couples therapy.

We went three or four times over the course of a couple months, but our couples counselor gave us some very strange advice. She told us that whenever Corey became angry and started yelling at me, that I should, in fact, stay where I was and engage. That when I walked out of the room to avoid a fight, I was actually emotionally abusing him by not allowing him to say his piece. I couldn't believe what I was hearing. I knew the fights were irrational and they wouldn't lead to constructive conversation. He would follow me from room to room, getting angrier and angrier. Nevertheless, I opened up to share my real feelings with Corey in those sessions. I let my guard down and let myself be vulnerable, and he pretended to be receptive in therapy. But after we left, he would use what I said to hurt me, because now he knew all of my insecurities. If he knew something he said particularly hurt my feelings, he would be sure to use that in later arguments, knowing it would hurt me the most. I used my last ounce of energy and determination to make our relationship work, and Corey was throwing my vulnerability back in my face like it was all some joke.

The last two months of our relationship were a roller coaster off the tracks that just kept plummeting down in a free fall. Corey was out of the house more and more, making plans with friends and coming home late, after I was asleep. I felt like he was acting out and trying to get my attention. We were on two completely different pages with different lifestyles, and our arguments were getting worse. We were both hurt, and whenever we argued there was no resolution. We might as well have been speaking different languages. And then I stopped even arguing. Nothing I could say or do would make him happy. I was defeated, and I stopped fighting it.

I was so numb and isolated and depressed. I felt like I had no one else, because I still didn't want to tell anyone what was really going on and how bad things had gotten. I was losing weight because of my nerves and the stress. Anytime I ate, I would start gagging and felt like my body was rejecting the very act of chewing. I couldn't keep anything down. I was wrecked on the inside and simply going through the motions on the outside. I felt lifeless. Kirra was the only source of light in my life, and I just tried to hold it together around her as much as humanly possible.

At first, I didn't say much to my parents about what was going on because I was humiliated. But they knew that something wasn't right as the frequency of my late-night visits to their home increased. I'd made the fifteen-minute drive to my parents' whenever I sensed Corey was angry or looking for a fight, which was more often these days. They looked at me strangely, and I know they noticed the dark circles and tired eyes, how I was losing weight from stress. I would hang my head as I opened their front door in the middle of the night with a sleeping baby in my arms.

My parents knew that I was struggling, but they didn't know the extent of it. I could usually make up an excuse for his absence and my exhaustion—he was traveling, or focused on work, or I needed babysitting help—and my parents would accept it.

But it kept getting worse. Sometimes I would stay with my parents for a week or two to avoid dealing with my relationship just a little longer. Kirra and I were always finding excuses to go to my mom's house for the weekend, or to go visit my grandma Betty. I knew I couldn't keep this up much longer, that soon Kirra would ask why we were going to her grandparents' house so much, especially late at night.

Almost a year earlier, Corey was coming down from a big party weekend with his friends, which meant following me around the house, yelling and accusing me of cheating on him with my trainer. I worked out with a trainer at 6 a.m. twice a week, and I was always home before Kirra woke up. Corey couldn't get this delusion out of his head—ironic, considering how often he cheated on me.

That night, I went into Kirra's room and locked the door. She was only a few months old, and I hoped that she was young enough that I could simply distract her with toys while I pulled myself together. But I couldn't hold it in, and the fear and the sadness burst through. I started to cry, really cry, tears streaming down my face as I tried to stay quiet. Little Kirra, with her big hazel eyes and straw-colored hair just growing in, reached over to pat my back. My sweet baby was trying to comfort me and show me love. My heart broke into a million pieces. Thank God she doesn't remember because she was so little, but it was only a matter of time before she started to notice that things weren't right.

Soon, I realized, she would be old enough to understand that her dad yelled, and we hid and ran to Grandma's house. I never wanted her to see me go through that or hear her dad treat me like that. I couldn't let her think this kind of behavior was normal or okay. I tried never to let things escalate while Kirra was nearby. I would defuse the situation or walk away, which drove Corey crazy.

That moment is what started the wheels turning for me to leave.

Slowly, because of my physical changes, my family figured out that something was up. My close friends started asking if I was okay, noticing my weight loss and sunken eyes from lack of sleep. I didn't want to talk about it. I'd married Corey, after all, and I didn't want to admit how bad things had become so soon after our wedding. By that point, to be honest, I was incredibly embarrassed that I was in this position, and that I hadn't made different choices when I had the chance.

For his part, Corey figured out that my parents knew we were in trouble, and he went to have a talk with my dad. In fact, he cried, and told my dad that he wanted to make things work. In the past, my dad had reminded him of his duties to take care of his family, and that he had to control his temper. I really do think that Corey tried after those conversations. I don't believe that his remorse and his apparent desire to do better were fake. But by that point in his life, he was who he was. He could only try it for a week or two before spiraling back into his old habits.

Finally, after staying at their house on and off for months, I did open up to my parents. Because of how often I brought Kirra over, I just couldn't hide it anymore, and the way they brought certain things up told me that they already knew, or at least suspected, what was going on. I was too ashamed to tell them exactly what Corey would say to me, or how I was feeling. Instead, I kept it simple: that I was unhappy, that he was mean, that he'd wake me up in the middle of the night to yell at me, and that he'd text me threatening things when I was out of sight. When I let my mom read what he texted me one time—a few cruel messages in which he called me names and made derogatory remarks about my life, my family, my friends—she got so upset. After the shock wore off, she was furious. We brought my dad into the conversation; he was also angry, but more levelheaded.

Both of my parents told me to walk away and insisted on helping out with Kirra while I figured out my next steps. They told me I had their full support and I shouldn't stay in a relationship with someone like this. Living the way that I was living, they told me, wasn't right and it wasn't healthy for me.

My parents' reactions weighed on me. My motivations for marrying Corey in the first place—to try to give Kirra the best, most complete family life possible—were still there, and I kept convincing myself that I could somehow crack Corey's code, as if I could dismantle the bomb before it went off. And then the three of us would have this hard-earned storybook life together.

In July 2017, I was invited to Miami Swim Week to show and celebrate Prey Swim. It was the make-or-break event of the fashion season for swimwear; all of the buyers and industry press were there to cover the shows, and it was my first time attending!

It was an incredibly exciting trip, and once I arrived in Miami, I had much to do to prepare for our first-ever runway presentation. We were showing our Fall 2017 and Resort 2018 lines, and we had last-minute decisions to make and model fittings to confirm. Fashion shows are a full production with lighting and music choices, and a lot of people to coordinate. I was eager to show what we had been working on and nervous to bring Prey Swim to such a big stage.

Despite Corey's track record watching her, I'd left Kirra with him while I was in Miami. The trip was short—just three nights—and Kirra was thirteen months old now. It could have been a huge turning point for my company, launching us into the next level of established swimwear lines—but instead, it became a turning point in my relationship with Corey.

The first day was a blur of preparations as well as some business meetings; yet as much as I had to do, I was also distracted by frequent text messages from Corey complaining that I hadn't taken him and Kirra along on the trip. I couldn't believe that he was giving me a hard time for a very short work trip, especially with how much he traveled.

My team and I went out to dinner to go over show details one more time, and to shake off our nerves with a good-luck toast. I posted our "cheers" moment on Instagram, and Corey immediately reached out to accuse me of partying instead of working. I tried to focus, but after dinner, when I reached out to Corey to check in on Kirra, he didn't answer. That's not exactly the most reassuring thing when you're away from your child.

Finally, a few hours later, he FaceTimed me from a friend's barbecue. It was dark outside, and I could hear people in the background. Kirra wasn't on FaceTime with him, and when I asked where she was and who was watching her, Corey's response was: "Don't worry about it." He hung up on me. I kept calling and texting, and he refused to answer. I was freaking out, to say the least, and it kept me up for most of the night.

The next day was the show itself, taking place on one of the many huge, tented runways set up for the event. I was so immensely proud of the designs and the work that had gone into creating the lines. And the show was a success! The designs featured a lot of subtle greens, blacks, and grays, and my favorite black-and-white gingham. With a classic hue, I often focus more on intricate silhouettes, lacing and ties, a lot of cheeky bottoms, or even a really fresh suspender-inspired suit. Walking out onto that runway to face the audience was such an incredible, surreal moment. It was a dream come true, really.

All throughout the day, I couldn't focus. My mind was consumed by the ridiculous, cruel text messages. He told me that I needed to get home *now*, accused me of cheating on him, and even said that if I didn't get back immediately he was going to kill himself. I was really worried for Kirra at that point, and Corey wouldn't give me an update on her, so I called my dad and filled him in. He immediately called Corey; when he picked up, Corey acted perfectly normal on the phone, saying that Kirra was fine. As he was talking to my dad, Corey also texted me—except his tone was very different.

I was so distracted by these texts as I was preparing to do a live press interview that I told my publicist what was going on, and that I had to get home. She saw me on the verge of breaking down, so she told me to smile and talk about how proud I was of the new Prey Swim line for just a few minutes, then after the interview we'd figure it out. I tried to remember my fabrics and my inspirations, to smile and to breathe, all while my mind was spinning, wondering if Kirra was okay. I was able to rebook my flight for the next morning. I just had to make it through the night.

The next morning, I finally got an update. Kirra had been coming down with a cold as I was leaving, and Corey sent a video of her coughing badly. I felt like I'd been electrocuted. He wrote that she was pretty sick and he was worried, and I encouraged him to take her to the pediatrician.

I was on the next flight out of Miami, and as soon as I got home and saw Kirra, I took her to the pediatrician right away. It turned out she needed a nebulizer for the next few weeks to get over her cold. That's how bad it was. After that, whenever I traveled for work, I always took her with me—no more exceptions. I would never forget the helpless feeling of being across the country from my baby, not knowing if she was okay. If it hadn't been clear before, it was now. Kirra was my only priority, and I would do anything and everything to make sure she was safe and loved.

Chapter Eleven

Don't Mistake My Kindness for Weakness

The last day of my marriage started like most other days. It was a sunny California morning in August, with the kind of bright, clear sky that just makes you want to get outside. I woke up early with Kirra, who was fourteen months old at the time and rarely slept past 7 a.m. I'd always enjoyed our quiet mornings together, lying in bed chattering to each other before heading downstairs to listen to whatever music she was singing along to at the time. I'd usually make breakfast for myself—avocado toast, or maybe some oatmeal—and share it with her.

That particular morning, I was heading out to work on my swimwear line and planning to take Kirra with me. I had a good, family-friendly office setup to run Prey Swim, and my family was always dropping by to say hello and to play with Kirra. I often took her with me, and she had some toys and books there. We had just gotten dressed for the day, and I was holding Kirra in my bathroom as I packed up a few things to take with me to work.

Corey had come in late the night before, at three or four in the morning after partying with friends, and he was sleeping it off downstairs as he had started to do, preferring to crash on the couch. Sometimes I'd tell myself that he did it so as not to disturb me. Mostly I knew that he just didn't want to see me—and that if he did, it wouldn't be for anything good. I had grown used to being woken up in the middle of the night by Corey standing over me, yelling and cursing things like, "You're pathetic! You're a failure! You're a fake cunt!" It's a startling experience, to say the least. After a few times, I'd learned not to sleep too soundly, to avoid the heart-racing confusion first thing upon waking up.

The night before had been one of those nights. Corey smelled of booze as he stood over me, shaking me awake. He was yelling in my face as I blinked my eyes open, trying to make sense of what he was saying, heart pounding. Before he left that night, I'd made a remark about him going out and meeting girls—nothing accusatory, but definitely said from a place of hurt and wanting to hurt. Now it was clearly stuck in his mind as he screamed at me, demanding to know who had told me he was cheating. I told him over and over that it didn't matter, that I wasn't mad, that he should go to bed. He finally relented and went downstairs to pass out on the couch.

You're probably asking yourself how I could possibly go back to sleep after such a jolting experience. The truth is, when something like that happens regularly, you just start getting used to it and developing coping mechanisms. I kept a journal by my bedside, and after Corey would leave, I would take it out to write. It helped me process my fear and anger and sadness, to get it out of my mind and body and onto the page. And then, slowly, I'd be able to go back to sleep. I'm not claiming that I was particularly well-rested during this period of my life, but another hour or two of sleep was enough to get me through the next day without crashing.

The funny thing about that night is that Corey wasn't wrong. I did find out about him cheating on me—*again*—through a friend of a close friend's boyfriend (one of those situations). I didn't really care. At this point, I knew he'd been cheating on me with random girls for years. I had stumbled upon naked pictures and dirty text messages in his phone; I had received tips and proof from strangers on social media; and I had heard it from his friends, who were there with him on the late nights and bender weekends. Just like the nighttime wake-ups, it hurt a lot at first. But now, having been with Corey for so long, I felt completely numb.

I was so focused on surviving day to day that it truly didn't matter what Corey did as long as it didn't directly affect me—or, more important, Kirra. I was living small, measuring my reactions, churning with unhappiness and loneliness, struggling with the fear that we would fight or that he would get angry. Anything that made him happier and nicer to me was fine in my book.

Kirra and I were almost packed up and ready for the day when Corey burst into the bedroom. We immediately froze, as if we'd been doing something wrong. He was already yelling as he came into the bathroom. "Tell me!" he screamed, face red and contorted in rage. "Give me a name!" He accused me of spying on him by talking to his friends. He was desperate to find out who'd told me he was cheating. He got closer and closer, his body changing as he got angrier. His shoulders squared, his chest puffed, his eyes widened and intensified. I felt like the bathroom was closing in on me.

I stood completely still. In a small voice, speaking as slowly and calmly as possible, I told him not to do this in front of our daughter. "It's okay, Corey. I don't care about the cheating. I'm not mad." I suggested I take Kirra over to my parents' house nearby and then we could discuss things once she was gone.

Without waiting for his response, I focused solely on getting Kirra out of the room. She was just sitting in my arms, eyes wide, looking back and forth between us quietly. I didn't want to risk upsetting her, so I remained as calm as I could. But before I could get to the bedroom door, he breezed by me and got there first, slamming the door shut to block our exit.

I could feel my heartbeat in my ears, and a shiver went down my spine as he squared his shoulders and narrowed his eyes. "Please," I whispered, "let me go drop Kirra off. I'll come back right after, but I don't want her to see this." I knew an argument was coming, and I wasn't even fighting it at this point. I just desperately wanted to keep Kirra out of it.

Corey grabbed the backpack I had been packing for the day and shook everything out across the room: my wallet, my laptop, toiletries, everything.

I took a small step forward toward the door, and he took a step toward me. Then he pushed me back with a hand on each shoulder. With Kirra in my arms. I stumbled backward, and, for a moment, I lost my breath from the shock. I held Kirra tight in my arms so she wouldn't fall.

I was barely able to breathe, shaking as I tried to calm Kirra, who was now screaming, eyes filled with pure terror. I felt my body course with the adrenaline rush of fight-or-flight.

Corey shifted and stopped yelling, maybe realizing that he'd gone a step too far, and started punching and hitting himself in the head. This just made Kirra scream louder. I was crying now too; I could feel the tears stream down my face even as I tried to hold them back.

After a minute of this fragile standstill, Corey finally calmed down and crumpled a little, exhausted and silent. He was so upset that his emotions were all over the place—angry, then crying, then self-destructive. As intimidating as this was, I saw my opportunity. I ran to the doorway of the bedroom, into the hall, and into Kirra's room, locking the door behind us. As I did that, I heard Corey leave the bedroom and pound down the stairs.

I wasn't sure what to do. Kirra stared at me with wide eyes, tears still running down her cheeks. Even in that moment of panic, I was afraid of people finding out how bad things were with Corey. I was ashamed that my husband treated me like this. I was embarrassed and sad that Kirra had to watch this, that she was in the fray this time when he'd pushed me. But my concern about the media weighed heavy, as much as it pains me to write that. I needed to protect myself—protect my daughter—from their scrutiny.

I shook off those fears and focused on our immediate safety. I called my dad first. Thank God he answered. I cried and ran him through what was happening. I asked him what to do, and his response surprised me. Calm and focused, he said: "Audrina, you need to hang up and call the police."

It was eerily quiet when I hung up the phone. Hearing those words out loud—from my dad, whom I trusted more than anyone—was gut-wrenching. And still, I knew I wouldn't call the police and risk this incident going public. Did I really feel unsafe enough to call the police? I wasn't sure where in the house Corey was, or what he was doing, and that unnerved me. Slowly and quietly, I opened Kirra's door.

Corey was right there in the hallway. When he saw us, he turned and ran down the stairs. There he grabbed a decorative metal vase on our console table and held it up to his head. Sobbing, he screamed that he was going to bash in his head in the middle of the street so that everyone could see it was my fault because I was going to leave him. I held Kirra in my arms, both of us crying as we stared at him in disbelief. I think I was in shock. Then, just as quickly, he switched tracks again—he wasn't going to kill himself anymore. Instead, he was going to spend every moment until the day he died working to destroy me.

I begged him again not to do this in front of Kirra. He wouldn't listen. In fact, he was just getting angrier and more out of control. All of a sudden, he walked outside, and I followed him with Kirra. I stood in the garage and watched as he opened the door to his truck. He seemed to have worked out some of his energy and calmed down. Looking right at me, he said: "Just know that this is all your fault."

And then he drove off.

I was dumbstruck. Was Corey going to hurt himself? Was that what he meant by saying it was all my fault? I felt sick. I held on tight to Kirra, and to that little glimmer of hope inside of me that wasn't yet squashed. And I waited. I waited for my family to come and help us like they always did. I waited for the white-hot panic I had felt to subside, so that I could finally think straight. I waited to feel safe.

The last two months of our relationship were the hardest of my life. Corey's temper seemed to be getting worse and worse, and each time we argued, it broke my heart and my spirit.

Truthfully, it was the emotional abuse that was really breaking me down. It was the things he would say to me, the names he would call me: "a cunt," "a bitch," "a messy, lazy woman," or even "a fuckup who's used by everyone and has no real friends."

I felt myself slipping away. The strength, the determination, the force of will I'd always relied on were replaced by his voice in my head. When you're told you're a piece of shit every day, you begin to believe it. It becomes your reality. You stop fighting back and slowly start to die inside.

With no bruises or scars, it was easy to deny what was happening. I chalked a lot of it up to his partying rather than an issue that existed within him. I would try to give him an ultimatum that he had to get professional help, to take anger management classes, and to work on himself, or I didn't want to be with him. He would agree, and I would return, but he never made good on those promises. Still, I made apologies for him. I spent a long time justifying his behavior and rationalizing how I ended up married to a man who could hurt me so deeply and so often.

And yet, here we were again. Only now things were much worse. I couldn't let my mind wander to what could have been if Kirra had been hurt. As I waited for my dad to arrive that day, I felt outside of my body as the adrenaline slowly worked its way through my system. I turned on some of Kirra's favorite cartoons and we sat together in the living room playing with her stuffed animals, dolls, and toys.

Finally I heard my dad walk in. I gave him the biggest hug and felt immediately safe, like I was a little girl again and my dad would fix everything. He just shook his head as he looked at Kirra and me, a little worse for the wear, but okay. We sat together quietly, playing with Kirra, not really saying much.

I recovered from that morning and, before long, Corey was back home. We kept going, with parallel but largely separate lives, which sometimes intersected. The next time they intersected a few weeks later, I did, in fact, call the police. I knew when the police came there would be no going back, and I was silently preparing myself for everything that was about to happen. I needed to do this—for real, this time. If not for me, for Kirra.

When two uniformed officers knocked on my front door, they introduced themselves and I began to tell them what had happened. It was terrifying to open the floodgates. I knew it would become public record, and eventually the inner shame of my marriage would be blasted all over the internet. But maybe being forced into the light to face the reality of my relationship and deep unhappiness was what I needed. Just saying things out loud did lift a little weight off my shoulders.

I knew the fallout wouldn't be easy. Nothing in our relationship ever was. But I couldn't worry about his reaction anymore, or what he thought.

This was never going to happen again.

I had spent years worrying about what people thought. The desire to please others drove so much of what I did—and didn't do—for so long. It's what made me cover up the problems in our relationship for years. It seemed like Corey knew that about me, and he learned how to use it against me. He exploited the seeds of self-doubt that had been sown over a decade earlier in the world of reality TV.

The entirety of my yearlong marriage to Corey was essentially a long, hard road to divorce. I felt shattered to my core after years of manipulation and emotional abuse, and the idea of facing paparazzi and the public's inevitable curiosity just made the process seem ten times harder. But I was finally forced to say enough's enough and end my marriage.

For the first time, despite all of the awful things that Corey had done to me prior to that, this truly felt like life or death. I chose life.

For the next few weeks after that incident—after the police came, and I filed the paperwork—Kirra and I stayed at my parents' house. Corey showed up a few times and begged me to come home. This time, I knew there was no going back. It was over. I had finally made the choice that took me years—and so much heartache—to make.

If you know anything about the court system and divorce proceedings, then you know it is an exhausting process. And this was just the beginning.

A few weeks later, in September 2017, I had to appear on a panel to promote Prey Swim in Newport Beach. It was actually a really cool, fun event moderated by Lydia McLaughlin from *The Real Housewives of Orange County*, and I was part of a roster of speakers featuring makeup artists Joey Maalouf and Susan Yara and 10.11. Makeup founder Erica Beukelman. It felt like my first return to normalcy since the incident, and I was really looking forward to it. Corey showed up at the event and came backstage to confront me right before I was about to walk onstage. He was obviously angry, and he chose this moment in a very public setting to confront me. The whole thing was terrifying and mortifying. He had been trying to find out where I was to confront me in person, because now, after months of avoiding any opportunity to take care of her, he'd decided that he wanted Kirra. He yelled at me, asking me where she was, demanding to see her, calling me all sorts of names. The hypocrisy astounded me, but it didn't surprise me.

While I was on the panel, I was totally out of my body, as if I were floating above myself and looking down at a woman in a black jumpsuit, laughing and smiling and sharing stories from starting her business. All the while, Corey was standing in the back of the crowd watching me, and texting me all of this crazy threatening stuff. My phone was backstage in my purse, so it wasn't until later that I read his messages. I tried not to focus on him, but he still knew exactly how to distract me and get in my head.

As embarrassing and awful as his now-public behavior was, it motivated me to move within days to obtain a temporary restraining order against him and actually file my divorce petition. I will never forget many things about that day I called the police, but something Corey said in particular stuck with me. He yelled: "Grow some balls and pull the trigger and file for divorce." Well, Corey, here you go. There was some sense of grim satisfaction when I served him with divorce papers in September, shortly before our one-year wedding anniversary in November. That satisfaction only lasted so long, before I found myself facing November 5—one year since our wedding—all alone. I couldn't believe all that the last year held for me.

Rather than formal court proceedings, my hope was that we could go to mediation to keep it all out of the press. As they usually do, somehow the paparazzi found out about our initial court appearances, and they were waiting for us at the courthouse. The prenup certainly helped us navigate some basics when it came to the divorce, but it quickly became clear that Corey was not going to go down without a fight.

To complicate things, Corey had been living at my house. Remember the house I bought while pregnant with Kirra in the perfect, family-friendly neighborhood? The one he wanted nothing to do with, so I bought it on my own, with my own money,

with my grandfather cosigning? Well, he got back to the house—
my house—first after the restraining order went through, and at
that point I couldn't get him out.

Soon Corey's parents flew out, and by the time we made it to
court, the three of them had been staying there for a few weeks.
There was nothing I could do about it except wait out the process.
I later found out that Corey went through everything, including
all of my personal belongings. He went through my jewelry and
paperwork. He even went through all of my journals that I had
been writing in all those nights he tormented me. He ripped the
pages out that detailed how sad and broken I was. There was no
reasoning with Corey. I was able to go back a few times with a
police escort to get clothes for Kirra and myself, a few boxes of
work files and products, and a few of Kirra's favorite toys.

As much of a violation as this was—and it made my skin
crawl, believe me—I was still out of the relationship, and I felt
freer than I had in a long time. I was truly so relieved not to be
in that house with Corey, or afraid of when he might come back.

Our lawyers negotiated on our behalf in mediation, and in
order to get him out of my house, I basically had to pay him off.
The lawyers came up with a settlement for me to pay Corey to get
him out of my house, even though it was mine, and even though
he had ransacked my belongings. I borrowed $35,000 from my
family to get the job done and paid my husband to leave.

Even with the restraining order, I was still very afraid of what
Corey might do. My biggest fear was, always, that I wouldn't be
able to keep Kirra safe. While he had taken over my house, he

went through all of my important documents and took both our marriage license and her birth certificate, among other things. I was terrified that Corey would find a way to take Kirra to Australia. If he could get a passport for her, he could take her on a plane, and I might never see her again. My lawyer told me that that kind of thing does happen, and if it did, it would be very hard to deal with. I couldn't let my mind go there. I didn't want to believe that Corey would do that, but I had to believe anything was possible with him at this point.

The very first night I was alone after the dust settled, back in my own house, I didn't know what to do with myself. I put Kirra to bed in her bedroom—the same room that had seen me at my very lowest moments and my very bravest, boldest moments too. I sat down, looked around the empty living room, and cried for a long, long time.

I was sad that my marriage had come to this, and that my daughter would deal with the ramifications of our relationship for the rest of her life. I cried as I thought: *How did this happen?* The answer was a mile long with the twists and turns of half a decade. I didn't want to be at this place in my life. I felt bone-tired from the years spent living on edge. I had lost twenty pounds just from the stress and emotions. But underneath the exhaustion and the sadness was something else: a huge sense of accomplishment, of triumph, that I had faced my tormentor and taken the steps to change my life that had seemed impossible less than a year before. I expected to feel a sense of peace without Corey, but I hadn't expected to feel so much more.

When I moved back into the house, I found a letter from Corey in my underwear drawer. He had apparently written it the night before, in his last night in our bed. He was emotional as he shared that he never thought our relationship would come to this. He wrote that he loved me, and Kirra, and he remembered some of our fond moments in the house. It was clear to me that he hoped this letter would be the first step in winning me back. It was so sad, in so many ways. The letter painted him as the heartbroken victim and guilted me about breaking up our family. It was hard to read, and for a moment this last-ditch effort at manipulation almost worked. I still have that letter tucked away in a box of memories and photos from my relationship with Corey. But I was out of chances. I was depleted in every way. It was really over.

My first order of business was putting the house on the market. I couldn't stay there anymore, for so many reasons. It was too big for just the two of us. I also knew that it was time to move on and move forward. There were too many ghosts haunting that place. It sold quickly, and Kirra and I lived with my parents for the next six months while we looked for yet another place to call home. During that time with my family, I focused my energy on trying to heal. I was in therapy, trying to get healthy and eat more and finally calm my nerves. Of course, I was making sure Kirra felt supported and loved too.

It was just where we needed to be. I felt safe, and I had help with Kirra as I took time to rest and to heal. We often ate dinner with my parents and siblings, and it was so nice for Kirra to be in that warm, high-energy environment. My siblings and extended family were always around, and Kirra was blooming with such loving attention. I am so grateful for that time and that support.

After six months of lying low, dealing with divorce proceedings, and trying to rebuild my strength, I knew it was time for us to move on. I was ready to have my own space and to create my own home for my daughter. I rented a little spot in Newport Beach, and Kirra and I moved there for a year.

Once Kirra and I were in the apartment, living on our own, it sank in for me: *I'm getting divorced. I'm a single mom.* It was so nice to have privacy and independence, and Kirra was enjoying her own room, full of her toys and books that had been in storage. It was small and cozy, and a great stepping-stone for both of us to adjust to this new life together.

As part of our divorce, Corey had been having visitations with Kirra twice a week for a few hours starting when she was fifteen months old. Because of the restraining order, the handoffs took place at the police station instead of at either of our homes. It was really, really hard to give Kirra over to Corey that first time, maybe the hardest thing I'd ever done. He hadn't been around, taking care of her day in and day out. Each time I would sit in my car as my mom helped Kirra out and took her over to Corey. My whole body would shake, and I could hardly take a deep breath to calm myself down. I couldn't even get out of the car. I was a mess.

Two days a week for a few hours at a time, it felt like my heart was beating out of my chest. I couldn't concentrate or think about anything other than Kirra's well-being. I was glad that

Corey's parents were there to help him with Kirra. Regardless of my personal feelings about them, they genuinely helped Corey, and Kirra loved spending time with her grandparents. Whenever Corey's mom was around, Kirra always came back happy.

Other times, however, when his parents weren't there, Kirra was introduced to Corey's girlfriend of the week. He had blocked me on Instagram, so I had friends keep me updated on anything he posted involving Kirra. Once someone sent me a photo that showed my little Kirra sitting on some random chick's lap on a boat, posted to Instagram like some happy family moment. That didn't sit right with me.

Thankfully, Kirra was young enough that the tabloid coverage of our divorce wasn't something I had to worry about her seeing. As soon as I filed the divorce paperwork, so much of what I'd been through became public information, including the events of that horrible day that started it all. I felt so exposed knowing that my life for the last few years was totally out there. People knew how I'd been treated. It's hard enough going through a divorce, but it's made even harder when everyone in the world can judge the intimate details of your life. As much as I didn't want the drama in our relationship to be public, the fact that it was out there was also a relief. I was no longer hiding what I was going through. I received a lot of support from my fans who'd followed my journey from *The Hills* to *Audrina* to the present on social media, and that meant so much to me.

I tried to stay silent and not give interviews. Paparazzi sat outside my parents' house for a few weeks, making it hard to leave or do anything, especially with Kirra. We developed a system where my aunt would come and park her car in the garage to sneak Kirra and me out. When we all left together, they wouldn't know which car to follow and we would get away unnoticed.

Slowly but surely, I was clawing my way back to myself in those days. I've always been kind and giving, but nobody should mistake my kindness for weakness. I'm not one to get in someone's face, and I tend to let other people dictate. I never put myself first. That might look like weakness to some, but let me assure you, I'm not wasting my energy stirring up drama that doesn't serve me. Instead, I choose to share my feedback with people respectfully, without hurting them. I let things go when they're not worth the fight. I'm kind and generous; I give people the benefit of the doubt and don't jump to conclusions; I prefer peace and harmony and fun. Until. Until my back is up against the wall, or until my daughter is brought into the equation.

Which is why, for a while, I'd forgotten that I can also speak my mind and stand up for myself when I need to. That strength had been chipped away over the years because of the slow and steady manipulation I had endured. But when Kirra was born, it reignited a spark in me. Slowly, when I became a mother, I realized that it wasn't enough just to put her first. I had to put myself first too, in order to be able to take care of her properly.

I think that's also helped me get in tune with my own intuition—the inner voice that knows the right answer or the path forward if you learn how to listen to it. I've faced some terrifying and difficult moments in the last few years, and I've had to learn how to tap into that intuition to stay calm and focused, to find strength to keep going and find a way forward. It's not easy to tune out all of the noise, the distractions, other people's opinions, and really listen to yourself. But you can do it. You just have to be quiet and trust yourself.

That's something I've been working on with Kirra too, when she gets really upset. I crouch down low, right in front of her, and say: "Okay, look at Mommy. Take two deep breaths, in through your nose, out your mouth. Put your hand on your belly and know that you are safe. You are here." It calms her down and by focusing on her breathing, she remembers that she is in control of—and safe in—her body. I want her to learn that she can control her emotions and her reactions to the world around her. I've certainly learned the hard way what an important skill that can be.

· Chapter Twelve ·

Another New Beginning

When I was first approached with the idea of rebooting *The Hills*, my initial reaction was no. That chapter of my life had been closed a long time ago, and I'd moved on. I felt like I'd lived so many lifetimes since the show first aired and I was an optimistic nineteen-year-old with the world opening up to her. But then I thought about the ways in which I'm different now, and the story I have to share with viewers—and I realized I actually had a lot to say. So I said yes.

As I was rebooting my own life, we rebooted the show. It wasn't always easy: I was trying my best to be happy and engage with the cast, but I was still so raw and shaken from my own personal drama that there were many moments where I would just break down crying on-camera. I never imagined that I would be thirty-five years old, divorced, and a single mom. I was slowly gaining my strength back, and my old self was reemerging mentally, spiritually, and physically. I was reintroducing myself to the world just as I was making sense of the last few years and getting a handle on my evolving identity. It was only as I was seeing the light of my new life and reconnecting with my old friends that I could see how dark my life had really become.

Right when we started filming in 2019, I moved into my new home. After my divorce, Kirra and I had moved in with my parents for six months, then to an apartment in Newport Beach for a year before I bought our house. When we finally moved into a home of our own—a cute and cozy bungalow that's just right for me and Kirra—I felt like I was waking up from a bad dream. I started to relax and feel like myself again. I had been so isolated that last year of my marriage, and during the worst first few months after our divorce, I was just focused on surviving.

In the toughest situations, I lean on my faith more than anything. I grew up going to church, and over the years I learned how to communicate with God in my own way. In my twenties, I would occasionally attend church with my family when I was in town, but not consistently. It wasn't until I moved back to Orange County when I was pregnant with Kirra that I started consistently going to a Saddleback church nearby. I felt connected to the pastor, Rick Warren, and I got so much out of his messages. In fact, he once talked about the power of the choices we make in our lives, and I've held that message close to my heart ever since. I joined in the small groups, read daily devotionals, and went to church pretty much every week. I took Kirra starting when she was small, and she's always loved it, particularly the music. Now I take her to a Sunday school class there too, which she seems to really enjoy. It's a nice community, and I'm so comforted to be a part of it.

In the last few years, I've found myself praying more than ever. As soon as all this happened with my marriage ending and struggling through the divorce, I really turned to God more than I ever had in my entire life. I was at rock bottom, and I felt depleted and defeated. I remembered that feeling I had as a kid in church, where I knew that no matter what, when it feels like I'm all alone, I can turn to God. When I was struggling in my marriage, I went to church every single weekend by myself. I would bring baby Kirra, and I would sit every Sunday, soaking in the comfort of my faith and trying to refocus my energy on God.

When I'm feeling dark or down or anxious, I try to focus on something bigger than all of us. I remember going in and out of the courthouse for divorce and custody proceedings, praying under my breath. Sometimes, if I'm performing or onstage to present an award in front of thousands of people, like at the Billboard Music Awards, I take a deep breath and say a little prayer. I try to let all that negative, scary, nervous energy out, and breathe in the good, positive energy from my faith in God.

When I watch those first few episodes of *The Hills: New Beginnings*, I hardly recognize myself. I was at the darkest, hardest point in my life. I was struggling to get back on my feet, and it was a slow, heavy process. Honestly, I tear up seeing how much I was on the edge of breaking down.

We all wanted this version of *The Hills* to be more genuine and more real than the original run, with more relatable insights and revelations about our lives. Basically the same show as before, just without as much scripting and editing. Of course, I don't have my daughter on the show, and there are certain aspects of my life that I don't allow to be filmed. But I try to share as much as I can, and I found new strength in being vulnerable.

It wasn't hard getting back into the swing of *The Hills'* "Audrina" after spending so many years away. I think on some level, I had been using the same skills I practiced on *The Hills* to protect my heart for quite a while in my marriage, pretending to be complacent and happy. Catching up with everyone would bring up all of these emotions and triggers—some good, beautiful memories to reminisce over, and some heartaches I'd almost forgotten about. It was hard not to get caught up in the intensity of what I was feeling. After a few weeks of filming, we all let our guards down and began to reconnect on-camera. Slowly I learned to open up and share real emotions. I learned the power of a good, genuine cry—even if it is on-camera. I learned how to be comfortable being me again.

It's funny to compare the two shows, because when *The Hills* ended in 2010, we were very different people. For the first go-round, we were young, wild, and free. The subject matter we were grappling with on *New Beginnings* nearly a decade later was undoubtedly more adult. Many of us were parents and talking about our children, our marriages, and, in some cases, our divorces, coming from a place of vulnerability and maturity. The fan response to the reboot—many viewers had been fans of *The Hills* and were catching up with us in our adult lives—was wonderful, and I received so many messages of support and thanks for sharing some of the difficulties I'd been through. There are always critics, of course, some of whom were looking for the antics of our youth—drink throwing, catty arguments yelled over club music, and the innocent optimism of dating in your early twenties. We were grown now, and *New Beginnings* shows that.

The last time many of us had seen each other was that big MTV wrap party eight years before. We had all gone our own ways, mostly outside of our former LA bubble. When we got together to start filming those first few days, we all kind of looked at each other and wondered: Where do we start? Do we hold on to the lingering dramas and resentments and pretend everything's okay, or do we let everything out and just go for it?

The answer to that question, for me, was complicated. I had begun to realize that I needed better boundaries in my life. I was learning to prioritize my own needs, and to put what works best for me first. It might sound simple, but so much comes down to the fact that I'm a people pleaser. I often push myself to say yes, to take things on, to help other people until I mentally, emotionally, and physically can't help myself anymore.

Setting boundaries is really hard in reality television. You want to make a good TV show, and there are all of these people in your ear telling you that if you don't do this, if you don't show up, then you're not going to get paid, or you're not going to be in every episode. It's complicated, especially since I'd set the precedent of saying yes. There were times I felt taken for granted, or betrayed, or disrespected by the producers. If I said no to something, I'd have two or three people from the crew calling me all day and texting me nonstop. I would get so overwhelmed and so stressed out that I found myself giving in just so they would leave me alone. Then I would regret agreeing to whatever it was and be so upset that I didn't stand my ground. It became one of the biggest training grounds of my life. I had opportunity after opportunity to learn how to hold firm and protect myself. Recently, I'm finally starting to get the hang of it.

In my real life, I'm trying to set boundaries too, even with family and friends, and learning to do things that are just for me and nobody else. I've learned that every time I give in or do something I don't want to, it's not as fun or fulfilling or worthwhile, because my heart's not in it.

The truth is, I wasn't alone in coming to *New Beginnings* with new baggage. The whole season was kind of heavy. A lot of the cast had lived through real, important moments and milestones, and the show was coming together as we all reckoned with what has changed and who we are now. It was a very emotional time for everyone. There were so many conversations where I opened up, particularly to fellow moms Whitney Port and Heidi Montag Pratt, about how I was feeling. That was the real me, reaching out for help and reassurance. It was heavy at times, but it was also very real—our goal in the first place. For the most part, I feel like it brought us all closer. Since Lauren had left the original show in the middle of the fifth season, there was no real expectation that she would be back for this show. At that point, we had our own lives on the show and plenty to say. Those of us returning had built real friendships. No matter what—through the good times and the bad times—it's like we're this dysfunctional family that will always have each other's backs. We might gossip about each other or call each other names within our circle, but no one else is allowed to do that, like siblings. At the end of the day, we're all there for each other.

I feel so lucky that the show has reignited some of my old friendships—and brought some new ones into my life. During the course of filming for the last two years, Brody Jenner, Frankie Delgado and his wife, Jen, and Jason and Ashley Wahler have become real friends whom I see off-camera. We'll go to dinners and hang out, and I'm comfortable sharing parts of myself and my life with them that I don't share on-camera.

When we started filming, I was so excited to reconnect with Heidi. We had hung out a couple times in the years between *The Hills* and *New Beginnings*, and we'd check in on each other here and there, especially around special occasions and milestones. Although we've had our ups and downs over the past few years, Heidi and I have the best time when we see one another. I've always had a lot of respect for her and Spencer. They put their marriage above everything else and are on the same team, always. Both of them embrace who they are, fully and without apologies; Heidi especially owns who she is—mistakes, flaws, and all. She's so funny and fun to be around. Heidi has always been heartfelt and honest about her life and experiences, and she's such a good listener.

Right away, I connected with Ashley Wahler and we went on to quickly forge a solid friendship. She's married to Jason, Lauren's infamous ex who asked her not to go to Paris. Ashley and I live close to each other so we would film together often, and we've spent a lot of time together off-camera too. She's such a strong woman and has been an incredible influence on Jason's life. I really admire her.

Both of these women actually listen to you and give you feedback that comes from their hearts. If you're in their life, they truly care about you. It was so much easier to speak with the girls I trusted. So when I needed to talk about a difficult subject, I would always tell the producers that I wanted to talk to either Heidi or Ashley in the scene.

As for me, I brought a sense of perspective and maturity to filming that I didn't have a decade ago. I now understand the difference between organic and manufactured drama, and I accept that producers sometimes need to push or plant the seeds of gossip to create a good show. Just like on *The Hills*, the producers of *New Beginnings* still have their storylines in mind and they encourage us to talk about certain conversations or fights, or certain people, depending on how they are pulling together the episode or what they need to be extra juicy. I don't have a problem with this, for the most part. I recognize the entertainment value needed in the storyline, and as long as it falls in the scope of my "Audrina" persona, I'll play ball. Parts of our voice-overs are more like true interviews where we can share our honest perspectives and give new insight into a scene. It's so refreshing to be asked to share my thoughts. But we don't know what the episode will end up becoming until we watch it with the world. I know not to take it personally. I've been in situations where something I said was clearly used to fit the desired storyline and dramatic arc of the show. As frustrating as that can be, I've been able to create some healthier boundaries this time around.

I also got reacquainted with Justin, whom I hadn't seen in years. After my divorce, he'd heard the news and had reached out to see how I was doing. Well, first I found out he was "concerned about me" from an interview he did promoting his band, but soon enough I heard from him directly. He was sweet, actually, and wanted to know how Kirra was doing. As a child of divorce, Justin was worried about her.

We filmed our first dinner together for the show, and it was such a shock to my system to be sitting across from each other with mics down our shirts and a camera crew in our faces, sparks flying. We caught up in between our flirtations. Our connection and our chemistry was still there, just as powerful and knee-weakening as always.

With his flirty smirk, he said about my marriage, "I don't think that was the love of your life." It's funny—in some ways it felt like no time had passed at all.

After we reconnected, there was definitely a flirtation there, but it was hard to know whether it was manufactured for the show, or if something real was rekindling. Just when I would feel good and optimistic about our potential, he would disappear for a few days and not call me back. I couldn't believe I was dealing with the same game-playing as ten years ago. The mixed signals never end.

I realized that Justin wasn't the right person to confide in anymore. My baggage was just too heavy, and I didn't want to put all of that on him. Reading in the press and hearing from me what went down in my marriage seemed hard for him to swallow. I understood then that it would take a strong man to handle my life. Justin loves to flirt and smile, and allude to what could be, but I knew it couldn't work out. It also came down to lifestyle. He was touring, partying, and having fun, and I was realizing that I needed to heal from my emotional trauma before I could even think about being with someone.

Looking back, at age thirty-six, I've only been in three meaningful relationships in my entire life: Justin, Ryan, and Corey. I may have dated them more than once, but what can I say? Once I let a guy into my heart, he's hard to shake.

Ryan reached out to me shortly after my divorce went public and the tabloids picked it up. We started talking again, and he was exactly what I needed at the time. Ryan has always been so loving and full of life. He brings such light to any room he walks into. We started hanging out again after years of not really seeing each other. Ryan was making me laugh and smile and feel a little bit lighthearted at a time that was otherwise so heavy for me.

I realized I missed having fun and I hadn't smiled or laughed that much in a long time. I could really be myself again. Ryan brought that carefree side out of me. He was always building me up and giving me compliments, and his positive outlook was contagious. He made plans for us to go to Disneyland, though I made sure it was in a group setting so I could bring Kirra along. I am definitely not ready to bring any man into Kirra's life yet. He also surprised me with a trip to Cabo for my birthday.

Ryan and I went to the Stagecoach music festival together, and we were at some daytime party there when a photographer captured us with Ryan's arm around me. The picture was published and the headlines called us an item. It might sound strange, but when we saw the photo, it sparked a conversation about giving it a real shot. I realized that maybe I hadn't given him a fair chance the last time we were together. We're both in such different places in our lives now, so I thought, *Why not?* He was always honest and treated me kindly and with respect. I think I was so used to being let down that I no longer expected anything from anyone. I was just happy to live in the moment.

At the end of 2018, I went to Santa Barbara with the rest of the cast for Heidi and Spencer's vow renewal, which was filmed for *New Beginnings*. There was some downtime during filming— we sat for hours as they filmed different takes, changed lighting, or adjusted camera angles—and at one point, I checked my phone and saw an email from my attorney. My divorce was finalized. I was overwhelmed, relieved, deeply sad. I had been waiting for over a year, so to have the process itself behind me was a weight lifted. Finally, I could move forward. But still, I was mournful. I wondered, *Did I give it my all? What would my life look like now if we'd stayed together?* I knew that I did everything I could to make it work, and it was so easy to romanticize the past.

Of course, I was also swept up in this beautiful display cele-brating marriage as I watched Heidi and Spencer affirm their love and commitment. I listened to the officiant talk about the power of love, particularly through hardship and difficult times, and I reflected on the end of my relationship. I was sitting next to Ryan, and that's when I knew it wasn't fair to him to keep seeing him. I knew then that I had a lot of healing to do, and I needed to learn to love myself before I could jump into something else. I needed to grieve the end of this relationship and, without distraction, focus on getting myself back on my feet. I could picture myself being with Ryan forever, and that kind of scared me. I didn't yet feel solid enough in who I was to really commit to someone else.

After just a few short, great months of hanging, Ryan and I went our separate ways. He was gracious when I pumped the brakes, as always, and I'm so grateful we've maintained a good friendship. He did bring up the fact that if I'd stayed with him back then, I never would have gotten back with Corey. While that may be true, I feel like everything happens for a reason, and obvi-ously there were a lot of lessons I had to learn from my marriage. (Not to mention: without Corey, there'd be no Kirra.) Ryan said that he would have taken care of me, and I could have pursued whatever I wanted professionally. It was meant with love, but I had just gotten out of an intense, suffocating relationship, and I didn't want to feel like I needed to be taken care of. I think a lot of women might have had a different reaction to that kind of offer.

Honestly, I haven't seriously dated anyone in a couple of years, not since Ryan. I've been on a few dates, but nothing significant.

When you have a child, it's not easy to date casually. Someone has to be really worthwhile for me to take any time or energy away from Kirra. And I'm not looking for anything serious, by any means. I've gone on a few dates for the show—with Sean Stewart, Rod Stewart's son, who appeared on a few episodes of *New Beginnings* with me—but that was just for the show. The producers want to see me putting myself out there and dating, so I go and I smile and I flirt. At the end of the evening, we go our separate ways. It's fun and low-stakes, and there are certainly worse ways to make a living.

I reconnected with actor and singer Josh Henderson, whom I've known for a while now, about two years ago when he started DMing me on Instagram, suggesting we hang out. I figured it would be fun, so when I was done filming the first season of *New Beginnings* and had some time free, I went to meet him somewhere in LA to play pool with a group of friends. I've always thought he was hot, but I've been pretty preoccupied in the last few years. When we hung out a few times, it was clear we had major chemistry. We spent a lot of time together, and we were calling and texting every single day. It was so fun to be into someone new. My favorite nights were the casual ones where he'd play music and sing, and we'd hang out with friends and play beer pong and relax.

We're very similar in a lot of ways, with overlapping world views. He avoids gossip and negativity, and tries to focus on the positive and having fun as much as possible. We also share our faith. We both are very connected to our faith and share worship music or readings that affect us. It was almost too good to be true. My lifestyle is just different than a single guy's lifestyle. I make plans in advance so I can get a babysitter. I prioritize family time with my daughter above everything.

Again, I kept my worlds separate. I tried to get Josh to do the second season of the show with me, but he didn't want to do reality TV. He was focused on his music. And, of course, I'm very protective of Kirra and keeping her out of my dating life. It's a lot for someone to take on, I get it. You just don't have a huge capacity for casual when you have a child.

I'm not sure what the future holds for me romantically. I don't know if I see myself getting married again. I battle with that possibility a lot. Sometimes I'm vehemently against it, and other times I feel receptive to it if I were to meet the right person. I guess the only true answer is that I'm open to seeing what comes next.

Justin once told me something after Ryan and I broke up that I'll never forget. He said, "You can tell when two people are meant to be together." I don't know if I believe that. I haven't experienced that kind of assuredness yet, but I'm hopeful that one day, I will.

I was thrilled to hear we would get a second season of *New Beginnings* after the success of our first season. I was in a better place emotionally another year out from my divorce, and I was ready to show viewers a much more balanced and upbeat Audrina. But remember that saying, "We plan and God laughs"? Well, a few weeks into filming season two, we were shut down when the Covid-19 pandemic broke out. It would be nine months before we resumed filming. While we were all separated during our quarantines, of course, I wasn't worried about how we would pick up the show when we could finally gather again. This group of friends has been tight for so long that I knew we would find our stride and reconnect over the shared craziness of the world. If anything, we would need even more of a stress release.

Brody and I had a chance to get even closer in season two. We're friends in real life, not just on the show, and that makes filming together so fun and so safe. We've spent a lot of time together, hanging out with our friends or listening to music, and sometimes just talking for hours, especially after a long day of filming. He knew what I had been going through, and he became someone I could confide in. We became so close that I came to trust him more than anyone else on the show. I knew he had my back, and vice versa. There was a lot of mutual respect and admiration . . . and maybe more.

One of the things that's burned me in past relationships is the desire to avoid the cameras and tabloid buzz, which this show very much creates. Sometimes dating actors and people who are too aware of the limelight can backfire. And yet dating someone outside of this world can be harder because they don't get it. Brody and I are very much on the same wavelength about how to exist in a world with paparazzi while maintaining our privacy and security.

And of course, production was up to their old tricks of trying to stir the pot, this time by trying to push me and Brody together. I think the producers saw our natural, flirty rapport and really wanted us to give it a shot, even going so far as to suggest we kiss. There's nothing more awkward than being asked to kiss in front of cameras when you actually have a little crush on someone. There's definitely something between us. It's not that I haven't thought about it—who wouldn't? He's gorgeous and sweet and soulful— but I value our friendship so much and I'm not looking for anything like that right now. I mean, we've kissed before, a long time ago. There are a lot of rumors that we've hooked up, and I get it—we'd be a damn fine couple. You never know what will happen. As a wise man once said, "Truth and time tell all."

The second season featured a few surprises when it comes to our changing friendships. Mischa Barton left the show after the first season, which actually didn't really surprise me. She had never seen the show before joining our cast. It was clear that she simply wasn't interested in getting into the drama. She gave it a shot, but it just wasn't for her.

I was surprised, though, that Heidi and I got into a very tense place. There was a feud between Heidi and Ashley, and I felt pulled into the middle somehow, which caused a lot of friction between us. The situation was so inane and immature, I won't bore you with the details—but it put me in an uncomfortable position between Ashley and Heidi. I was really hurt by Heidi blaming me for an issue she really had with Ashley. I found myself surprised to see Heidi act in such a way. It was heartbreaking. There had always been blurred lines between our on-camera and off-camera friendships, and this bled into our off-camera friendship in a big way. These kinds of situations are often manipulated and made worse by production, but now our real friendship was at stake. Again, I learned to keep my work separate from my personal life. I started to pull back from my friendship with Heidi, and keep it professional. I do what I need to do on-camera, but that's it.

When Kristin Cavallari came to town for a cameo in the second season, I caught her up on the situation with Heidi. Kristin agreed that it was so petty, and we both decided that it wouldn't stop us from all hanging out together despite the drama. I saw Heidi at a party and I finally had the chance to confront her. I was too adult to let these things simmer. I went right up to her to address the issue, and that broke the ice. We were able to connect and talk it out off-camera. It ultimately became a breakthrough for us, and we're back to where we were and moving forward.

No matter how long the show runs for, I hope that this incredible group of friends can make the effort to stay close. We all have so much going on—with growing families and businesses and demands on our time—but what we have is special. We've been through so much together over the years, and I'm determined to stay close.

Recently, I also had a chance for another new beginning: relaunching Prey Swim. After Miami Swim Week, my divorce got underway and I couldn't afford to keep the business going. I was self-financing instead of taking on investors, and it was too expensive to pay for that and legal fees. So I closed up shop to focus on pulling my life together and healing after the divorce.

Now I'm in the process of relaunching Prey Swim. I'm so excited to work toward expanding the brand to loungewear and basics, beach accessories, and the whole beach lifestyle. The design process for the expansion has been so rewarding. I've looked at beaches around the world, from my own travels and those of my friends, searching for inspiration from different beach cultures. When I'm building a collection, I choose the pieces, colors, and patterns that I'm drawn to and would wear myself. I consult with my friends on their body types and preferences to create pieces that drape beautifully and fit like a glove. I wear T-shirts most days, and I was finally able to design the perfect T-shirt in classic black and white, and in my favorite colors to add a pop to my outfits. It's all about the fabric—thick and smoothing without being *too* thick. I won't tell you how long I spent perfecting the neckline and the length of the crop.

Designing and running Prey Swim ignites and challenges me, and it makes me feel so accomplished. I want to expand into accessories and even into kids' wear, so Kirra and I can coordinate. More than anything, I do it so Kirra can see me put my mind to a passion and successfully follow through on it.

· Chapter Thirteen ·

The Fighter

*I*t's been a long and winding road that led me here: from the incredible highs of getting cast on *The Hills* and living the life of a young MTV star with the world as her oyster, to the lows of feeling lost and broken by a relationship that dragged me down for far too many years. I've learned more than a lifetime's worth about love, heartache, identity, and staying true to yourself. I try to look back on the last several years with love and gratitude. Although they were the hardest times of my life, they also gave me the greatest lessons and the greatest gifts, chief among them my daughter.

I spent years telling myself that things would get better if this thing happened, or that thing happened, until I finally realized the only thing I could change was myself. I could say, "Enough." I could leave. I learned you can't ignore things and just hope for the best. I never wanted to create drama, so I tried to let things go, to back off. But what I ended up doing was perpetuating a cycle of bad behavior and disrespect by silently nodding and accepting negativity. I trained myself to smile instead of scream.

For so long, I fought for things that were a waste of my time. Finally, I see the light. I know right from wrong, and I know what's worth fighting for. I don't care about people-pleasing anymore, or relationships that are dragging me down. If something's not meant to work, then it won't work, regardless of how much time and energy you pour into it. I was such a fighter that I fought for all the wrong things—even the things that I should have given up on. I'm not making that mistake again.

What I've been through has made me look at my life, and at the people and situations in it, so differently. It's made me truly appreciate what I have. It was only after I became a mother that I started to see that how I was responding to the world wasn't good enough for my daughter. I learned the importance of standing up for myself. It also forced me to listen to my inner voice and to pay attention to my gut instincts. For so long I'd ignored the little signs and the worries, hesitations, and uneasiness I felt in my life. And now I know better. If I won't have my back, who will?

It took me a long time to find the strength to get out of my relationship, longer than I care to admit. There were so many signs, both big and small, that I didn't listen to, including the sound of my own inner voice telling me it wasn't right. I didn't want to let anyone down, so I kept denying those fears. Those little moments kept building and building, and ultimately erupted.

I will never again ignore my own instincts, my deep desires, and my true needs.

Looking back, I still don't entirely understand all of the ways I put myself in emotionally destabilizing and damaging situations. I have spent some time trying to understand Corey and what could have caused his behavior. I could speculate, but the truth is, I really don't know, and I'm going to stop trying to clarify and rationalize his unforgivable behavior. In the end, I can only speak to my intentions and my heart. Why did I stay? I wanted to love him, and to be loved by him, and I wanted my daughter to have everything she deserves in this world, including a solid family and a doting father. But we don't always get what we want.

The hardest lesson for me has been the importance of loving yourself. It sounds so simple, but when you don't love yourself, you don't want to be loved. You try to push the people who do love you away. You're willing to settle for less, and you often attract other people who don't love themselves, and who pull you down as they struggle to stay afloat. You don't see the good in yourself or your life.

I strive to surround myself with people I trust to remind me of who I am when I stumble. It was so easy to get caught up in the fast-paced energy of working and traveling, just listening to people because they're well-known or seem cool. I found myself going with the flow too often, not wanting to upset the crowd and the status quo—even if I wasn't comfortable. I believe that if you don't learn your lesson, you're going to keep circling back to it until you do, going through versions of the same events with different people until you can finally open your eyes to what to do differently. Every day is like Groundhog Day until you learn how to fix your mistakes.

Maybe that's why I kept going back to the same men over the last decade. On and off with Justin, and Corey, and even Ryan. I never closed the door entirely, even when it was seemingly over, or actually dug beneath the surface to learn from those relationships. I now know that when someone showed me his true colors . . . I should have listened. Through words and actions, people show you who they are. Don't ignore red flags simply because they obscure the perception you have of someone, or of the relationship you'd like to have in a perfect world. Because the truth is, a relationship isn't going to solve your problems. Before you can really love someone, you have to know and love yourself. Sometimes relationships actually bring your personal problems to the surface even more. I knew I was unhappy, but I didn't know what I wanted in my mind or my heart. That's something I've worked at realizing in the last year or two.

It wasn't just my relationships, though: at nineteen years old, thrust into the spotlight on the show, I had a lot of people in my ear telling me how to act, how to dress, what to say, and who to date. There were so many outside voices coming in louder than my own. I was thrilled just to be in Hollywood, building a career, so I did the scenes, I followed directions, and I bent myself in a thousand different ways to become someone else. Now I've stripped away all of that pretense. I'm finally at the point where I know who I am.

Writing this book has been one of the most challenging undertakings of my life. It has been incredibly emotional and often difficult to relive so many moments from my past that I've tried to forget, and to put it all down on the page in black and white. It's also been therapeutic in many ways, and I've had to step through my fear to put this part of me out into the world. I worry about judgment and what people will think of me—one little person more than anyone else. But I'm being completely honest. This is me. This is my story.

It's also important to note what I'm not doing. I'm *not* writing this book to put anyone down or to speak poorly of them. This is my journey, and I'm reckoning with my choices and my experiences. Everyone has their own story to tell. If anything, I want to thank the people who have pushed and challenged me in my life for making me stronger. Despite everything that I went through, I am who I am today because of it. Maybe you can't ever really know what has made someone else who they are; all I know is that I can't change other people. It took a long time, but I had to let go and do what's best for me.

Part of owning who I am means taking responsibility. There's no one to blame for anything that I've been through but myself. The choices you make in your life are everything. Every day we can choose to love ourselves, to honor ourselves, and to live by our hearts and values, not by the outside pressures. Those are the most important choices of all.

In looking back and facing my past, I realize that I was the one forcing my marriage to happen. Once I found out I was pregnant,

I felt a sense of obligation to create a family even though I had reservations about my relationship. I should have stepped back and took Corey's behavior for what it was. He was showing me who he was even though I tried to deny it. If I had listened to my gut, I would have saved myself a lot of pain and heartache.

I'm blessed beyond belief to have had the opportunities and experiences that I've had in my life. I know that, and I could have written an entire book about the joys and blessings in my life. But instead, I've focused on some of my biggest challenges here to show the choices and the life-changing moments that made me who I am. I share this vulnerable side of myself in hopes that it might inspire readers who are facing some similar hurdles. To help readers understand that this kind of slow emotional destruction can happen to anyone—even smart, successful, capable women—and that there is so much joy and beauty on the other side. And for one little girl in particular, I hope she finds wisdom and hope in reading these pages one day, and that she never struggles in the same ways I have.

What I want to share with Kirra and every woman out there is that you have to put yourself first. Don't rush into a relationship if you're not ready; your timing is important. When you're uncomfortable, unsure, or unwilling in any scenario, use your voice. I want all women—Kirra among them—to get comfortable saying no without excuse, apology, or explanation. We have a right to say no when we aren't 100 percent sure. We don't owe anyone anything.

For women struggling through toxic relationships and abusive situations, I see you. I've been you. I wish it were as easy as me telling you that. The truth is, there's no one magical moment or mantra that will break the spell and release you. You have to want to live free more than you want to live easily. It will be hard—maybe the hardest thing you've ever done. I'm still going through it, and it's a constant battle, mostly against myself.

I get messages all the time from women who want to know how I got out of my marriage, as if there's some secret that I can pass along. I have never given specific advice because I wasn't sure that I had anything to offer. But after reliving this journey, I feel confident that I've finally learned a few things:

- **Listen to your instincts.** If something doesn't feel right, it's not. If an opportunity, a relationship, a friendship, or a business deal makes you a little uneasy, walk away. If you feel compelled to say something, do it. Listen to that intuition. Don't bite your tongue.

- **Let go of fear.** Fear keeps you stuck. Fear of being alone, fear of a relationship falling apart, fear of disappointing people. It keeps you treading water in an ocean you don't even want to swim in.

- **Stop caring what other people think.** I learned the (very) hard way what people-pleasing can lead to. I spent too long caring more about what other people thought than worrying whether I was really, truly making myself happy. *You* come first. Put your oxygen mask on before helping others.

• **Dream big.** Take the shot to accomplish your dreams. I'm now expanding my swimwear line into a beach life-style brand, which fills my creative and entrepreneurial cup daily.

• **Hold your power.** After years of getting my feelings hurt by the nonsense on the show or in uncertain relationships, I finally realized that I was giving too many people access to my heart. You choose who you let in, whose opinions and desires really matter to you.

• **Stay focused.** It's so easy to get sidetracked by the drama and judgments swirling around us. Remember your priorities, stay on track, and don't waste your energy on distractions taking you off your path.

• **Surround yourself with the right people.** Resist getting sucked into a world you shouldn't be in. Look for people who build you up and have your best interests at heart, and hang on to them no matter what.

I tell Kirra something a lot, and I think it applies to many of us. When someone is being mean to her at school, I say: "Remember that how someone treats you and how they're acting out is because of what they're going through, not you. Try not to take it to heart." I want her to know that other people are going through things we may never know. It doesn't excuse their behavior, but it helps to know that it's not always about us. And it's not our job to fix them.

I'm walking a very different road than I ever imagined I would, but I remain strong for Kirra and for myself. I am my only way out of this situation, and I will fight for us every day of my life. I work on myself every single day to continue to heal from my damaging relationship. I continue to see a therapist, I exercise almost every day, I go to church, and I listen to music. I try to do simple, healthy activities and make healthy choices, and I surround myself with good people. As long as I'm staying on the right path every week, reading daily devotionals or inspirational stories or anything that will open my mind and make me look inside, I just constantly try to learn about myself and discover what I want. I'm digging deeper, and I'm slowly transforming. I feel like I'm coming back to myself, stronger and lighter and more peaceful than I've been in a long time.

I've cut a lot of people out of my life as a result of all of this, which is hard. But I'm not in my twenties anymore, and I'm not interested in the party lifestyle or the bullshit. When you clear out the negative or toxic people from your life, it makes more room for the positive, encouraging people. I have friends in my life now who are also working on themselves and willing to engage in deeper conversations. They bring out a really positive side of me.

Strangely, the Covid crisis over the last two years has been a blessing for me because it's made me stop and slow down like never before. I had to sit with myself more than ever this year. Kirra and I have had some amazing, quiet days together at home, and I've felt really, truly present. It's been a tragedy for many, many people, but in many ways, for me, it was an unexpected gift.

The last few years have been some of the best, most joyous and love-filled of my life, and also some of the toughest and most soul-shattering. I've had to learn how to stand up for myself, how to use my voice and advocate for what's right—which all comes down to the fact that, even in my darkest hours, I'm a fighter. That's something I will never let myself forget again.

I've done my best in these pages to share my darkest moments and the lonely road back to myself. I hope more than anything that someone out there will feel a little less alone as a result. No matter who you are and what you struggle with, never lose sight of who you are. If I can share the ways in which I summoned my strength to inspire a few readers in their own lives, it will be worth it.

So while this isn't the way I thought my life would end up, when I think of my girl sleeping sweetly in her bed, my loving family supporting me, and the continued excitement I feel to pursue my dreams, I know that I'm blessed, and I know that my future will be bright.

We all have the power to create lives that we love and relationships that fulfill us, and to explore our potential and passions. I am choosing the people I let in and those I spend time with more carefully than ever. I'm choosing the projects, the work, and the energy that I bring into my life. I've finally realized my value and my right to be treated with respect, kindness, and compassion. I'm teaching Kirra about the power to choose, and how when we wake up, every day is a new beginning.

Afterword

A Letter to Kirra

I know that one day Kirra will be old enough to ask for answers. She'll probably Google her parents, and she'll likely read the years-old tabloid coverage of our relationship. I'll try my best to give her answers based on her age and what's appropriate for her at that time. There's no opportunity to hide my past from her, and I'm realizing I don't want to. Instead, I shared myself in this book for her, so she could know me in this way—as an imperfect but evolving woman—and so she could learn from what I've been through. If anything that I've done helps her to make better choices, then I would do it again a million times over.

Kirra,

I know that one day you'll read this book, and that fact has given me pause more than anything else when it comes to writing my story in such raw detail. There are things in here that I'm not proud of—moments when I should have been stronger, days when I ignored my gut instinct, and years when I let myself accept something less than love. I'm still working through so much of what has happened, but here are the things I know for sure:

You are so loved. Kirra, you are the reason for everything. There is no doubt in my mind that your father and I were meant to be together even for a short while to create you.

You are strong. I remind you almost daily to speak up, to ask for what you want, and to know what feels right and wrong to you. I want you to know the power of your voice.

You have made me a better person. Becoming your mother and loving you in a way I have never loved before changed me deeply, and opened my eyes to see life in new ways. I don't live for the drama; I live for the peaceful mornings with you at home. I don't worry about the haters; I worry about your well-being and keeping us both healthy and safe. I don't care what people say about me; I care about what we say to each other so that you feel seen and loved every day.

I want you to know there will be hard times in your life and struggles we can't yet imagine. You might find yourself in a relationship that's not working, in a job that's stifling your potential, or frustrated, overlooked, misunderstood in some other way. There's nothing I can do to protect you from that. But I can prepare you to know who you are and what you're capable of, something I can already see. I will do everything in my power to make sure you never forget the confident, beautiful, bright little girl you are now. I will show you by example how to never let your inner voice go unanswered and to never let your voice be ignored by the world.

Love,
Mama

· Acknowledgments ·

To my longtime people, thank you: M.S., L.K., A.B. You've always had my back, and we've been through it all together. Thank you for your encouragement, your guidance, your endless support!

My wonderful editors, Natasha Simons and Maggie Loughran, whose incredible vision and editorial skill helped *Choices* come to life. To the whole team at Gallery, thank you for believing in me and this book.

Thank you to Kirsten Neuhaus and Ultra Literary.

To Jen Schuster, thank you for your guidance—both editorial and spiritual.

And my family and friends, always, thank you from the bottom of my heart for the support and encouragement.